SLITHERIN' 'ROUND TEXAS

A Field Guide for People Who Dislike the Snakes of Texas

by

Jim Dunlap

Illustrations by

David B. Howard

Republic of Texas Press
an imprint of
Wordware Publishing, Inc.

Library of Congress Cataloging-in-Publication Data

Dunlap, Jim.
Slitherin' 'round Texas : a field guide for people who dislike the snakes of Texas / Jim Dunlap : illustrations by David Howard.
p. cm.
Includes bibliographical references and index.
ISBN 1-55622-313-7
1. Snakes--Texas. 2. Snakes--Texas--Identification
3. Rattlesnakes--Texas. 4. Rattlesnakes--Texas--Identification.
5. Snakes--Texas--Humor. I. Title. II. Title: Slithering around Texas.
QL666.U6D85 1993
597.96'09764--dc20

93-34488
CIP

1506 Capital Avenue
Plano, Texas 75074

Printed in the United States of America

ISBN1-55622-313-7

10 9 8 7 6 5 4 3 2 1
9310

All inquiries for volume purchases of this book should be addressed to Wordware Publishing, Inc., at the above address. Telephone inquiries may be made by calling:

(214) 423-0090

Contents

Part II — The Rattlesnakes

To my sister
Paula Jean Mischel

Acknowledgements

There is not a book on the shelf that was not written with the help of many people. That assistance might not be in a mechanical or informational way but in the form of encouragement, emotional support, and sometimes agreeing just to move things along. I am grateful to those people who answered endless questions, showed me where to find something, pointed out a detail, corrected my mistakes, and just helped out in general.

I tell my colleagues, and they agree, that my memory is about thirty seconds long. There are some people who come to mind who have contributed to this book whether they knew it or not. Thank you Ardel Mitchell, Jim Murphy, Terry Hibbits, Jim Stout, Alan Tennant, and Dave Blody. Then there are my colleagues who put up with me like Peggy Terese, Geri Kelly, Sally Evans, Fran Oubari, Kathie Schafer, Melvin Kirkum, Bobi Lastinger, Sharon Dubois, Jan Stevens, Kim Davis, Andy Sharpe, Donn Simons, Audrey Webb, and uh, let's see, who else?

I'll borrow a line from a good friend and Texas history writer, Wallace O. Chariton, who requested he remain anonymous, which is strange because I thought he was Presbyterian! If I forgot to thank you and you have your copy of this book, please write your name in the space below. Then if we ever meet like thieves or ships in the night or some other way, just bring it to my attention! I'll be happy to sign the book as authentication that you did help.

Forward

Let's face it folks, the snake got bad press from the Bible times of Adam and Eve and it has been going down hill ever since! I have spent a lot of time in my life listening to snake stories. It is difficult to find a tale that does not include the phrase "the one that almost bit me!" I realized that field guides, species accounts, herpetological papers, pet guides, and even children's books are hardly recreational reading for most people. I have never seen a snake book on a coffee table! It is also very hard to make snakes entertaining. Snakes don't do tricks, so you won't find one in the street act of a clown in a theme park.

Information is the key to allowing snakes to exist in this world without every Tom, Dick, and Frank wanting to wipe them out. So, with that in mind I wrote this book. My thinking is that if you pick up a book and right away you read something humorous, you might read on. Most of this material is worded so as to sound, for lack of a better term, "silly!" But, while you were not paying attention I have slipped in some facts.

Over my forty years with snakes I have "almost stepped on" and "almost been bitten by" just every about species of snake in Texas. As a child I collected and studied them as a hobby. When the smell of gasoline and perfume hit me as a teenager I acted accordingly; but I kept my snakes.

The memory of my first encounter with a snake is a bit fuzzy. Now that I think about it, the incident may be the reason my memory has always been a little fuzzy! I attended school in what was then a small rural district. I was in the second grade at the time. I remember that particular year because it was the same year that the school almost burned to the ground. I had nothing to do with it! Where were we? Oh yes, the snake. It was recess on a hot Texas afternoon. I was hanging by my knees upside down on the monkey bar. Just swinging along in the hot breeze and enjoying blood running to my head, I noticed something on the ground. I stopped swinging and stared. There was a small head poking out of a hole in the ground near where the bar met the dirt. It was a small snake. I got so excited, my first thought was to apprehend that snake. I went for it! I forgot one minor detail. I was hanging upside down by my knees! I let go and the ground came up very quickly and collided with my head. I don't remember ever seeing the snake again and that is understandable. He saw eighty pounds of red-headed, freckle-faced, t-shirted, blue-jeaned, bare-footed, second-graded human falling toward him at the predetermined law of physics rate of 125 miles per hour! It was time to leave.

I have dealt with animals all my life and I am lucky in that I do not really fear any of them.* It is not my goal in this book to eliminate your fear of snakes. It might be dangerous if you suddenly decide that all snakes are sweethearts and you grab the next copperhead you see in the driveway. I only want you to realize that snakes have a place in the natural scheme of things. You may not be convinced to help them, but maybe you will just leave them alone.

*I am real nervous around dogs!

Author's Note

Yes, I know this is a book about snakes. And yes, I know that there is a time and place for everything, but as a teacher I would feel amiss if I did not share some information that I believe to be fraught with import and pregnant with meaning. In my book *CRITTER CHRONICLES* I advised readers about the humane trapping, removal, and relocating of some diminutive denizens of the domicile. In other words how to get rid of squirrels, raccoons, and skunks. Since that publication I have found a new method. I would hate to think you might go through life and not know about fox pee!

For the past year or so I have advised callers to travel to their local sporting goods store and purchase something that might be called a "Deer Hunter's Kit." Within this kit there is a bottle of (small tiddle or short guffaw here) concentrated fox urine. I have had numerous re-calls attesting to the success of using this stuff. I finally decided to buy a kit just to see what I have been recommending. I called and asked for sporting goods department. "Bud" answered. Trying my best to be tactful and sensitive (after reading this book you will know how tactful and sensitive I am!) I described the stuff to Bud.

Bud listened quietly while I waxed very scientifically about the product. He responded with a very succinct "Oh, you mean Red Fox P." Uh, yes. That's it.

Well, I bought some. I am writing exactly what it says on the label: ORIGINAL, Tink's RED FOX P, Cover Scent, 100% RED MEAT FED. *Real Red Fox Urine, full strength, helps you get close to your game. *Use with Tink's #69 Doe-In-Rut Buck Lure. *Packed in Glass. Sealed in Wax.

Seriously, folks, this stuff works. Just a few drops placed near the hole made by the squirrel or raccoon and you will never see them again. This product is only available just before deer season.

I do have a few questions for the manufacturer. Where do you get your foxes? How many foxes does it take to fill a vial? How do you get them to fill a vial? Can you convince them that this is just part of a routine physical? Do you have to run water in the sink?

CAUTION: Do not use this stuff around the deck where the skunks have taken up residence. The smell puts them on the defensive and they spray everything!

Introduction

This book is intended for people who are charter members of the PWAUROS Society. That stands for "People Who Are Unduly Rough On Snakes!" I might also start a club for "People Who Are Unduly Rough On Shower Curtain Rings!" You know who you are. You're always pulling the shower curtain off those little plastic rings and then lying about it! Uh, sorry. I have a tendency to wander. Back to snakes.

Here is the problem. You are cleaning the pool when lo and behold there is a snake in the bug trap! You are gardening and move a stone to get at a pesky root. The root turns out to be a snake! You are edging the lawn and the edger blade flips a snake right up in your face!

At this point some questions quickly come to mind: What kind of snake is it? This may be because by then you have put a remarkable amount of distance between yourself and the slithering thing. Or, you have reduced the serpent to a small smudge of what looks like avocado dip on the end of your rake handle!

Will it bite? From your present vantage point, that being the next area code, or just standing there with hoe in hand and avocado dip dripping off the blade, this seems to be a moot question. Perhaps it would be more correct to ask, "Would it have bitten?"

Is it poisonous? Of course it's poisonous, it's a snake isn't it? The triangular shaped head, the flat body, the beady eyes and you could tell right away it was out to kill you.

Can it outrun me? You have answered that question by now if the snake is not slithering along beside you. Or, it doesn't really mean anything to the snake because he has already passed into snake heaven!

Are there more? You know in your heart that there is a nest of snakes nearby and they are poised for revenge. If you have already dispatched the critter, you have heard the story about his mate tracking you down and going for your throat!

Then there are those of you who will ask really meaningful questions, like: What does a snake eat? How does it grow? What lighting, how much moisture, what temperature does it like? How does it normally obtain food when it is not invading your home turf or can't use the telephone to order pizza out? What eats snakes? How do they protect themselves? How many kinds of snakes are there? How do they reproduce? Are they hardy, long-lived, fast evolving, strong swimmers, good to eat, fun to play with, socially organized? If those are your questions I suggest you try another book!

As an educated, really with-it consumer, you will try to get more information. If this knowledge is not for your own safety and piece of mind, think of it as an effort to save the rest of the family and a couple of neighbors from certain death. So, you call "Snake-busters," i.e., your local friendly zoo or nature center. You call and give them your right-on, precise, nail-on-the-head, accurate description of the terrible beast. The person on the phone tells you that your snake could be anything from a harmless grass snake to an escaped Australian viper-cobra-bushmaster-rattlesnake-something-or-another!

That is not good enough for the safety of mankind so you attempt to locate a book. The NATURE section of the local bookstore seems to be the place to go. The name of this book is something like *All You Ever Needed To Know About Texas Snakes*. In this book there are at least four beautiful color pictures of different looking snakes all with the same name! None of these pictures look anything like the creature that almost attacked you. The utter frustration may cause you to sell the house or at least keep an extra watchful eye on every corner of the place.

The first thing you might notice about *Slitherin' 'Round Texas*, is that there are no beautiful color photographs. I look at it this way. If a snake scares the beegeebees out of you in the first place, why would you want to look at a book full of beautiful color photographs?

It would be very helpful if, after catching a mere glimpse of a round patch of snake that was quickly disappearing under, around, or over something, you could use this book and maybe come up with a positive identification. I would like for the information in this book to give you specific data like: Order: squamata, Family: Colubridae, Genus: Elaphe, Species: quttata, Subspecies: quttata. Age: 3 years, Length: 427.5 cm. Weight: 678 grams. Nonpoisonous, Probable Destination: mine, the next county; his, snaky heaven! But alas, that ain't the case. The best I can hope for in this book is: Ratsnake, won't hurt you! Or, if all else fails, you could throw this book at the snake!

The second section of this chronicle is devoted to the famous rattlesnakes of the Lone Star State. I have gone to the trouble and a great deal of expense to highlight those snakes that some Texans are convinced are the only snakes in the world. You will find everything you would want to read about rattlesnakes. If just that word "rattlesnake" is all you care to know about them, don't go any further than Part II, page 113.

Format

"Mary had a little lamb. Its fleece was white as snow!" I have this feeling that I could continue that narrative and nobody would ever notice. I may be wrongly assuming that everyone reads a reference book the same way I do. I tend to skip over all the stuff at the front of the book. And, I do not read instructions until I have flipped almost every page and I still can't find it!

The following is a brief description of how each snake description is arranged. It will detail the kinds of information you will find in the narrative. I would most likely just turn to the section and take my chances. It takes me much longer to find things than most people.

The introductory paragraphs will be garnished with personal experiences — both mine and that of anyone else! You might also notice a potpourri of bad jokes and worse humor. What can I say?

The color key that follows in a few pages only mentions two main colors. The second area you will read in each section will offer a detailed description of the color or colors you might expect to find on this particular snake. You must realize that colors will vary among individuals of the same species. Most of the variations involve lighter or darker color. There are a number of snakes that change color entirely between juvenile and adult.

The pattern is the logical characteristic you would look for after establishing the color. This characteristic is subjective and I will attempt to weed out matters of opinion. It is necessary to establish my own standard of pattern. If you do not agree and he bites you, I hope I was wrong and you were right!

In my former life I spent eight years as a policeman. After working a number of traffic accidents and crime scene investigations I noticed a strange phenomenon (thank goodness for Spell-Check!). The descriptions were as different and numerous as there were witnesses. One person would see a 5'3" suspect where another witness to the same incident would see a 6'0" suspect or dog or light pole. I have tried to compare size with some inanimate object that we all have some common interpretation of its size. For example: Most of us know the length of a yardstick. Some of us can visualize the diameter of a broom handle or a number 2 Berol pencil.

Lifestyle and/or behavior is where I try to rely on personal experience as much as possible. My grandaddy told me that if you believe everything you read, you shouldn't read! What does the snake do when he is not out attacking people. If he is not on your garage floor threatening the very existence of your cat, where is he? Foraging for food or water, sleeping, resting, eating, gathering with friends for a hiss or slither session, etc. You will find a little of that here.

Toward the end of the entry I will discuss similar snakes. This is not a redundancy. Of course they are all similar, they're snakes! When two species are pretty close in color, pattern, occupy the same habitat, or have the same behavioral tendencies they will be listed in this section. Sometimes this might lead to an identification of "could have been either one." That will cause no harm if the snake in question is nonpoisonous. The description will be very detailed if that is the case.

Last but not least I will include a brief geographical range. These are based on actual specimens that were collected in the area. These captures or sightings are recorded by county. There are some records where one animal is located far from the rest of the population. These are assumed to be transplants by means of releases or hitchhiking snakes.

For those of you who have already discussed the snake encounter with a friend, relative, or total stranger and have come up with a common name, the snakes are listed in alphabetical order. Look him up and read on!

Colors and Patterns

Let's face it, what might be red to me might not be red to you. Snake haters have a further problem because they don't care what color the snake was. I have never known an art teacher that could agree with me about a color. To avoid this conflict I think I have come up with the solution. You will notice the chart on the next page has a number of blank rectangular boxes. Each box has a color named below and a number. Don't panic! These are "colorless" boxes so you have not gone color blind. Try this. Borrow your kids' big box of map pencils. It might be easier to use the Crayola crayons but the wax rubs off and might mess up the back of a page. Read my color and then choose your version and just color in the box.* If that is what you think red is, so be it! Oh, one other thing. If you are sensitive, creative, dance well, and have a great personality, you might want to add a little to your life. You may feel free to add "ishes" to each of the colors!

So here is the trick. You will choose two colors each with a corresponding number. The result being you will have two numbers that indicate the primary and secondary colors of the big bad snake.

FIRST COLOR: You have now caught a glimpse of the big nasty snake. Right after your entire life passes before your eyes, you should see a color. There should be more of this color than any other. Don't lay a dead snake across your color chart or you will get ghastly things on the page!

SECOND COLOR: This would be the color of spots, stripes, blotches, patches, bands, heads, tails, or anything else on the snake with color.

You should now have two numbers in mind. I read an instruction booklet on how to assemble a jungle-gym so I know what I am doing! For example: The number 16 would indicate a snake that was mostly brown with some white in there some place. Should your sneaky snake be a solid color the second number would be a zero. The number 70 would indicate a green snake.

* You might notice that all the cartoons in this book just cry out for some color. Go for it!

COLOR CHART:

Brown — 1	Tan — 2
Orange — 3	Red — 4
Black — 5	White — 6
Green — 7	Yellow — 8
Grey — 9	Blue — 10

PATTERN:

Now that we have established a color, we must identify a pattern. Pick one you like!

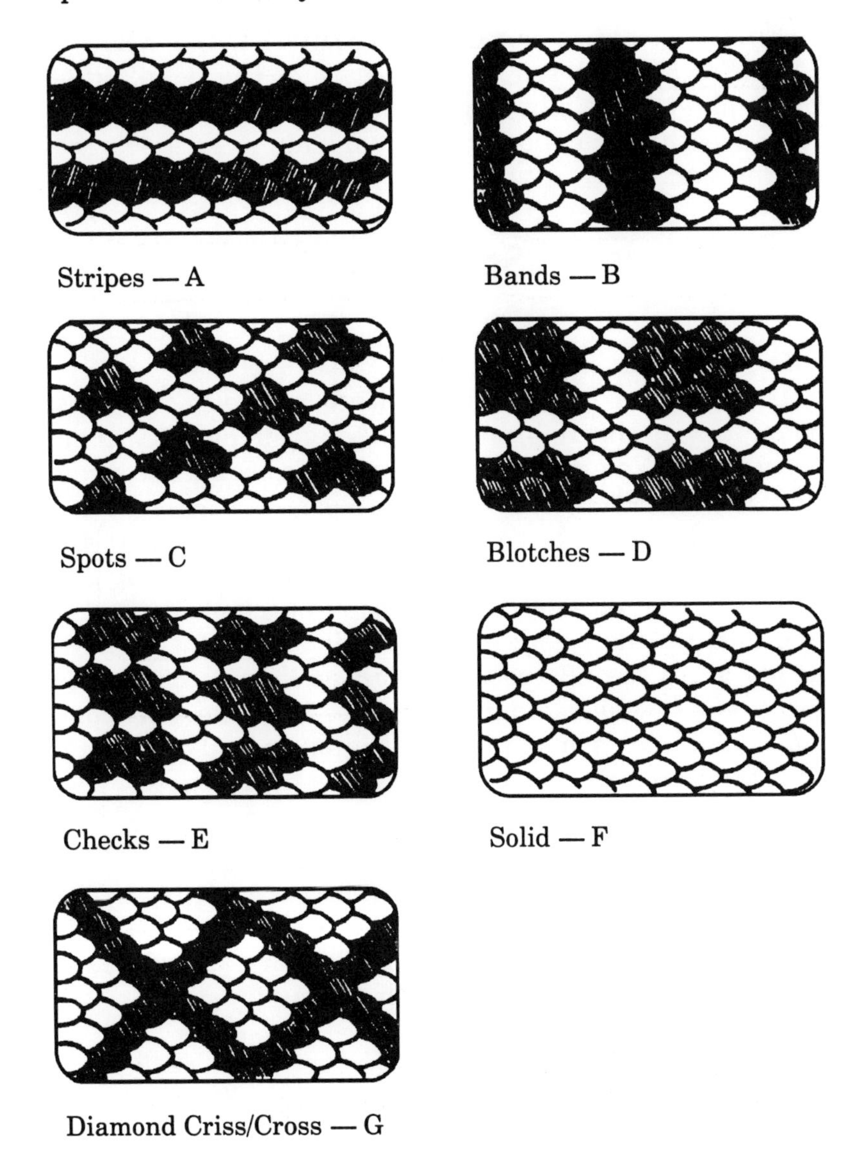

Stripes — A

Bands — B

Spots — C

Blotches — D

Checks — E

Solid — F

Diamond Criss/Cross — G

I have always used an old acronym as a self-help when I put anything down on paper. It is called the KISS principal. That means, Keep It Simple, Stupid! So now you should have two numbers and a letter in mind. For example: 51A should mean a black and brown snake with stripes.

Find your set of numbers and letter in the following SNAKE KEY and you will see most of the possibilities. Every single possibility can be found in this list. Not so, scale breath! Move along to the page numbers for further information.

Snake Key

*DISCLAIMER:

If you are a herpetologist, either amateur or professional, taking this information with a grain of salt will not be sufficient. You might want to read this book while straddling a salt lick!

To find the snake you have chosen just look at the following number/letter and consult the proper pages. I have assigned an identification code to each of the snakes described in this epistle. Keep in mind that this is by no means all of the 68 species of snakes known to occur in Texas. Narrowing the number to just 24 of the most common snakes took a lot of research, planning, and hard work. I want to thank the person or persons who did that!

First number	main color
Second number	secondary color
Letter	pattern
SAMPLE:	56A would be a black and white snake with stripes.

Find the number and letter combination on this list. Turn to the page number that follows and read on!

All of the possible number combinations would require something on the scale of "How To Win The Texas Lottery" so work with me on this. There will be codes that fit more than one snake. If after you have read all the descriptions listed with that code you still can't tell the difference, move to Alaska. No snakes!

OPHIDIOPHOBIA

Webster's Seventh New Collegiate Dictionary defines ophite as serpentine, snake-like, akin to, and so forth. When you add that to phobia, we all know that means "snakes scare the hell out of us." By one estimate, as much as one-fifth of the population of the United States suffers from some degree of ophidiophobia. It is right up there with fear of heights and enclosed places. As with all fears, there must be a million reasons we use to justify their causes. From personal experience, I can say that almost every individual with a fear of snakes is a victim of society. We were not born afraid of snakes! You can't use that excuse for a number of other things, although we really try.

Let's face it: snakes have gotten bad press even in the Bible from Adam and Eve. The fears and fallacies of snakes have been on the rise ever since.

An example that I use in classes to point out an improper introduction to snakes serves many purposes. In my introduction, I build up to actually looking at a live snake by searching around in a large styrofoam container for a bag. I remove the bag and at the same time talk about harmless snakes. I act surprised when the bag is empty. I look back into the big container, seemingly looking for an escapee. Very dramatically, I lunge forward grabbing for some unseen serpent. I pull out a large rubber snake and quickly force it at my throat. I choose my audiences carefully, because I don't want someone to have a seizure.

"I start off with the word "rabbit" and wait for a reaction!"

This circus show stunt illustrates a number of points. Number one is that it is certainly no way to meet a snake. Number two, I really enjoy it. And number three, it could be used as a harsh but somewhat effective laxative!

I am and have always been a student of human behavior. One of my little experiments always seems to have the same result. I establish eye contact with someone and softly but firmly say a word. I start off with the word "rabbit" and watch for a reaction. I then go to some other furry little mammal, like "guinea pig" or "monkey." The reactions with these words can be summed up by just saying Awwwww! My next word is, of course, "snake." The reactions follow a predictable pattern. First, the eyes widen. Pupils dilate. I lose eye contact. Slight panic is evidenced by twitching motions, sudden movements, the quick look around, and usually the exclamation, "Where?" After I have assured the victim that there isn't a snake within a hundred miles of us, I ask for first thoughts. Although it varies slightly, I usually hear phrases like, "Where's the hoe?" "I need a big rock." "Have you got a stick?" "Get my gun," and some other expletives deleted.

As a child, I introduced a number of people to snakes by tossing a dead one at the back of their necks. My victims were usually little third-grade girls running on the school playground. I found later that little girls are not really afraid of snakes. They just run screaming to humor the silly little boys! That, of course, is one of the wrong ways to meet a snake.

"Then they slowly worked their hand down my hand to the snake."

I have been successful in desensitization when it became necessary for a student to stay in my classroom for the remainder of a school year. The first step was discussion. We would simply talk about snakes and try to establish the facts. For example, they learned that snake skin is not slimy, but may be cool and dry to the touch; that many snakes are really sweethearts by nature; and that they flick their tongues as a means of smelling. We then took the "acid test" where the student was encouraged to approach the locked top aquarium snake cage. We then worked around to actually touching the snake with a gloved hand. Sometimes it was just too much for the student to touch a snake so I would talk them into touching my hand as I touched the snake. Then they slowly worked their hand down my hand to the snake. After the first few weeks I had "former" ophidiophobics sitting through class, ignoring my lectures, holding a snake in their laps.

Removal of all fear might be dangerous because I certainly would not want them to approach a rattlesnake in the pasture and get bitten. But, we reduced the fear enough to make it through the school year with flying colors.

After you read this book maybe you will be like the guy who broke his arm. He asked his doctor if he would ever be able to play the violin again. The doctor said he did not see any reason why not. The guy was thankful because he had never been able to play the violin in the first place! That is the dumb joke of the year but I am very fond of those!

You can enjoy nature without having to keep looking over your shoulder for fear of a snake attack. Watch out for those dogs though. They have big teeth and are unpredictable!

Scientists, and you know who you are, don't seem to know any more about what causes ophidiophobia than they do about any other psychological or emotional disorder. They do, however, know enough about treating the symptoms so as to bring about a "cure." Psychologists are people of "jargon" so they have come up with some pretty scary and expensive terms to describe goings-on down at the old doctor place. On the bill you might see — systemic desensitization, symbolic modeling, deep relaxation and symbolic modeling, deep relaxation and guided participation, and others. The truth is that all the treatments for these big worded techniques are as simple as talking!

Besides dogs there is one other fear that I have. Each morning it is my job to feed the cat. The cat eats from a bowl on the back porch. I am a creature of routine so I do the same thing every time. With an open can of "mystery meat" cat food in one hand I open the screen door. I put one bare foot on the porch and lean out to dump the gunk in the bowl. I have this fear that one morning I will step out and my bare foot will come in contact with a giant slug! The thought of all that sticky goo oozing between my toes just makes my fillings hurt!

POISONOUS VS. NONPOISONOUS SNAKES (La Difference!)

There are certain noticeable differences between poisonous and nonpoisonous snakes. But, when you look at the physical characteristics that indicate this difference there is a big problem. The average snake hater does not have the time nor the inclination to get that close! All of those differences can only be seen from a distance of a few inches! Let's look at two distances from which to view sets of characteristics. One we will call "SAFE" which means these characteristics can be seen as you bolt in a different direction, as you crumple to the ground in a dead faint, or from across the street. The other we will call "UNSAFE." Unsafe will apply when you are eyeball to eyeball with the snake. At this point the eyeball may be the only thing recognizable after the severe smashing you have just administered.

Physical: These cannot be seen from a distance and are considered unsafe.

1. Elliptical pupils. For those of you who don't do that word "elliptical" just think of a cat 's eyes. I personally would not get that close to a cat. Most of the harmless snakes have round pupils.* (NOTICE the asterisk here and go look for it!) The pet shop variety snakes such as boas and pythons have the cat eyes and yet are nonpoisonous. Are we confused yet?
2. Facial pits. Snakes don't get acne so we are talking about a small hole located on the face between the eye and the nostril on either side of his head. These heat sensing pits can be found on the rattlesnakes, copperheads, and water moccasins. These snakes are

usually referred to as "pit vipers." I guessed why almost right away. You can't get anything by me! These are absent in harmless snakes.* (Here it is again!)

3. One piece anal plate scale. I'll save you a trip to the GLOSSARY. The anal plate consists of one or two scales that are located near the underside of the snake's tail. This is where he goes to the potty. Most harmless snakes have a divided anal plate scale. The poisonous ones have a single scale. Some analogy can be made between boxer shorts and briefs but I can't put my finger on it.

Behavioral: These characteristics can be observed from a distance and are considered safe.

1. The poisonous snakes usually stand their ground and harmless snakes move out quickly. If you are already in the "catch hat" mode, this may not be of any concern to you!
2. Poisonous snakes will try to impress you with an eye catching defensive display. For example the water moccasin will open his mouth wide in a yawn (that's no time for you to take a nap!). The copperhead will flatten his body and freeze. The rattlesnake will coil and rattle. Don't count on the coral snake to do anything fancy. He just lays there and looks colorful.
3. Most poisonous snakes have a triangular shaped head. This is a good one if you don't really care. Do not use it if you are about to be forced into a close situation with a snake. A common harmless rat snake in a defensive position will flatten its head and the shape is just as triangular as a rattlesnake.
4. Then there are those that will try to fool you. The harmless rat snake, when cornered, will coil, hiss, strike, and vibrate its tail. To the casual and terrified observer this looks just like the actions of an upset rattlesnake! The harmless hognose snake will flatten

his neck like a cobra and hiss loudly. If that doesn't work and you touch him anyway, he will roll over on his back, loll out his tongue, and for all practical purposes act like a dead snake! The harmless bull snake will puff up and let out a hiss that will make you check all the tires on your car for leaks!

The safest way to treat all snakes is to stop, look and listen. If you can see a snake, just back away slowly and leave the area. You should not draw and fire. If you hit a friend you may not go to jail but you might die of embarrassment. It is a bad idea to go get a stick and come back! It is even worse to go gather up some friends and bring them back! Snakes are small and frightened easily (like you care). They just want to be left alone. Or to borrow a line, "Can't we all just be friends?"

* There seems to be an exception to every rule. The coral snake, which is poisonous, has a divided anal plate, no facial pits, round head, and round pupils. If you have been paying attention, those are the characteristics of a harmless snake.

PART I
Non-Rattlesnakes

TEXAS MOST SEEN SNAKES

Blackhead Snake

There are five species of black headed snakes that occur within our boundaries. With just a few well-chosen words and without a net I can tell you all you care to know about this nemesis of the leaf litter.

The solid color body ranges from light grey to darker grey. It should not come as a surprise, but this snake has a black head! He is the diameter of a pencil and averages eight inches long. The diet consists of small stuff such as centipedes, worms, spiders, insects, and their eggs and larvae.

The blackhead snake likes it moist so he stays beneath rocks and loves to be in deep debris. My wife told me if I did not quit pecking on this keyboard that I would be in deep debris. I'll move right along.

This is a laid-back little reptile and does not bite humans. During the heat of the Texas summer he will go underground and take a long nap. He is so small that the hot sun can turn him into what looks like a piece of beef jerky in just a little while!

The Plains blackhead snake is the most common of the five species and is found over the central and western parts of the state. What are the names of the other four species you ask? We have the southwestern blackhead snake, the Mexican blackhead snake, the Devil's River blackhead snake, and the blackhood snake. There, now I hope you're happy.

Blind Snake

From a distance this is, for all practical purposes, a worm. If you get closer, you will notice that it is a peculiar looking worm. He might make his appearance while you are bustin' clods from the flower bed. He is nonpoisonous and much too small to bite a body part.

An average size would be 3 to 5 inches but they have been recorded up to 11 inches. He is the diameter of the lead of one of those jumbo pencils. The eyes have become useless little black dots which appear to be buried beneath the scales.

This snake has a light cream colored belly. The back is light tan or dark brown with no pattern. When attacked by ants or a frightened gardener this snake has the ability to cause his scales to tilt slightly. This gives him a shiny silver color. Along with that he will writhe frantically and coat himself with feces and a slimy substance from his anus. The slimy stuff is thought to act as an insect repellant for use when he invades ant and termite mounds in search of food. I have been meaning to contact the "Off" company and see if they are interested.

If the blind snake ever surfaces, it is usually under the leaves, rocks, or dead logs. He burrows in search of ant and termite eggs, larvae, and pupae. The tail is tipped with a tiny spur. He uses it to act as an anchor to push his head and body through the dirt. Somebody might accuse him of having a stinger at the end of his tail but don't you believe it!

There is only one other snake in Texas that might even come close to looking like this snake. The New Mexico blind snake looks almost exactly like the Texas variety. For the life of me I can't think of a reason you would want to know the difference!

You might find this critter anywhere from the Red River through Central Texas all the way to the Rio Grande. He would be a novelty in East Texas, the Panhandle, and the Trans-Pecos.

Brown Snake

I grew up calling this little critter a DeKay's snake. It was not that I knew personally the man who is given credit for naming it that, but someone in my dim past just told me what to call it. I have never seen one of these crawling around on top of the ground. I would always move leaves, logs, rocks, and everything else out of the way during my snake hunts and this one was always under something.

If you find yourself moving trash or other piles of stuff from one place to another, you might cross paths with this snake. These are called "city snakes" because they like to live near us. The color of this snake will vary between all the "ishes" around brown. The one distinguishing color I use is the large blackish patch on either side just behind his jaws. He has two parallel rows of dark colored dots that go from the back of his head to the end of his tail. This arrangement would be classified as a striped pattern if you are at a distance and the only part visible is what is left outside the rock you just dropped on him!

He has a plain belly that will be light colored. The young have a distinctive yellow collar across the neck.

This is one of your "dinky denizens" and hardly ever grows to over 10 inches. They are about the diameter of a pencil and if you imagine the eraser, it kinda looks like a pencil!

These snakes will flatten their bodies when you bug them, as if a 10-inch snake could intimidate a big human being. You're darn right he can! And, as if you would ever notice, they will secrete a foul smelling liquid from scent glands located the same place where they go to the bathroom if you pick them up. The odor is not particularly offensive unless you spend a lot of time scratching your nose. This snake has been reported to flatten its head and bare its teeth. If you carry a very large magnifying glass with you everywhere you go, this might get your attention!

When dinner is on the table these snakes prefer a meal of slugs (they can't be all bad), earthworms, and soft-bodied insects.

This snake looks somewhat like the ground snakes, worm snakes, ringneck snakes, and baby garter snakes. All of these are nonpoisonous and much the same.

This snake makes his home throughout central and eastern parts of the state. He is a stranger in the Trans-Pecos area and the western parts of the Panhandle.

Bull Snake

I topped the hill on a country road and noticed a large bird sitting on the center line. I slowed from 83 mph down to about 10 mph and didn't even squeal the tires. The bird noticed me and began to flap. At first I thought he was stuck in some hot tar because he was getting nowhere. He then slowly gained an elevation of about three feet. He still seemed to be tethered to the pavement by a big rope. I drew closer. I know that is not a very descriptive statement but it just sounds funny. Anyway, I drew closer and noticed that the bird, a large red-tailed hawk, was trying to make off with a road kill bull snake. I could have said any kind of snake here but I am a truthful person! The bird started down the center stripe as fast as his wings would carry the rather large and long bull snake. I followed. I didn't clock his speed but he was moving faster but still remained at elevation:three feet! Then he took a right. The tail of the snake, plus about two feet of body, bumped along the shoulder of the road, across the freshly mowed weeds, and into the top two strands of the standard five-strand bobwire fence. (Should this book make it anywhere up north, I should have said "barbed wire" fence.) The tail of the bull snake wrapped around the top strand of wire like a bullwhip around a clothesline. The bird was either determined to get that meal or just surprised. He was thrown to the ground with an undignified smash. He stood up, looked around as if to say "that didn't happen." He was headed south soon.

Let me introduce "Mr. personality," the bull snake. As soon as he is aware of your presence he will puff up, open his mouth, and you will hear the loudest hiss you have ever heard. At the same time he has elevated the forward portion of his body in an s-shaped curve. Most of the time before you take the time to say howdy, Mr. personality has been identified as a lowly rattlesnake and has been reduced to ground meat! I think he gets his name from the fact that he is mostly "bull." This action will vary greatly between bull snakes. Some will allow themselves to be handled and never raise a hiss. I knew you would want to know that.

Think about French's mustard. It is not that yellow but in fact it is an "ish" of yellow. That is the main color of this snake. He has black, brown, or reddish brown blotches along his back. His belly is yellow with black spots. The belly may be all you can see from your vantage point on the other side of the barn.

His pattern can best be described as blotchy-backed from tail to head or head to tail. Depends on how you look at it.

This snake is one of the largest of our Texas snakes. He grows to a little over six feet and is the size of your wrist. He prefers to dine upon small rodents that he scares out of holes in the ground. He is not above climbing trees and raiding bird nests and eating the eggs and/or the babies. It is an egg-laying, nonpoisonous, good-to-have-around snake so don't kill it!

Opinions are like noses, everybody has one, but I really don't think there is another snake in Texas that looks like this one. You might think you have encountered a western diamondback rattlesnake with a slight case of yellow jaundice by his actions. He fits everything but he is nonpoisonous and has no rattle.

The bull snake is a resident of all but the eastern one-fourth of the state.

Coachwhip

I was standing in line at the grocery store the other day and it was the longest slowest moving line simply because I was in it! The person being checked out was participating in a ritual that I will never understand. The clerk was working as fast as she could and this person was just standing, waiting, looking around, fiddling with fingernails, etc. The clerk announced the total. Then, and only then, did this person begin to "unpack" to look for the check book. These people never pay cash. In the midst of the search this person turned to ask if I happened to have a *Mastigophis flagellum* on hand. To which I replied, "but of course!" I am asked that same question in grocery store lines all the time!

We all know that the person was inquiring about the beautiful coachwhip snake. The coachwhip gets its name from the long woven appearance of its tail. Folklore has it that if you grab this snake, it will whip you into submission with its tail. This is not true but it looks as if it could happen.

I know that this stuff does not fit the bit but it has been bothering me. There are two things I would like to see in grocery stores. The sign that reads, "Limit Nine Items" should be changed to read "We Will Check Out All You Can Carry In Two Hands." And, there should be a small counter off to one side where people could unload and reload purses, billfolds, backpacks, and other personal containers. Do these people think that their groceries are going to be free? This counter could also contain a good set of reference books for people with snake questions. How's that for relating?

"The coachwhip gets its name from the long woven appearance of its tail."

The coachwhip is a hyperactive, nonvenomous fighter and biter. He gets so frantic he will strike past your hand and go for the body! You love him already, don't you?

The color of this snake will vary with the main background color of the habitat from which he originated. You know that cat and dog owners seem to start looking like their pets. Well, there is no connection here but I think that's funny! If he lives on the grey limestone of the Edwards Plateau, you will find a silvery colored snake. The red mud west of the Pecos will produce a red coachwhip. This snake made a mess of my color chart because he is one solid color for the head and neck of his body length and another color for the other. Take note here that snakes have a definite neck and tail. He is not tail from the head back!

Let's just consider two colors, grey and red. If his head is dark grey then he will tail-out at light grey. If his head is dark reddish brown (are you following me here?), he will lighten up as you look toward the tail. The young are brightly patterned with a light main color and dark patches all down their backs. There is a exception to the color rule if you live in East Texas. There are always exceptions to everything if you live in East Texas! The coachwhips there are mostly black.

If the colors give you a fit, there is a distinguishing characteristic. If you have the opportunity to get face to face with this creature and you are still conscious, look at his eyes. Those eyes are big and he has a perpetual frown on his face.

The average adult size reaches from four to five feet and is the diameter of a broom handle. The young are about a foot long when they hatch and about the diameter of your pinky finger.

The coachwhip is not considered a city slicker. He prefers the dry countryside where he hunts during the day and sleeps in a hole or under something at night. He will dine on mammals, birds, and reptiles, and the young will devour insects and worms. He takes a chance being a daytime hunter because the big birds of prey (hawks, falcons) just love "coachwhip au gratin."

The two species in Texas, the eastern and the western, look exactly alike except for the color. I might add here that they are fast. You won't see much but rest assured that he is trying to put distance between you and him.

Crayfish Snake

We could get into a discussion about that name right away. Is it crayfish, crawfish, or crawdad? This is about snakes so we will worry about that some other time. If you have seen him at all, it was moving through the short grass at the edge of the stock tank. Uh, excuse me just a minute. Ah, that is much better! I have on a new t-shirt and that little nylon tag on the collar was sticking me in the neck. It must be folded under until it is washed a couple of time to soften it up so I can stand it. I think if you cut it off, the secret service guys will come around and wrestle you to the ground. Or, maybe that is on cushions. Oh well.

I am sure you grew up calling this a Graham's water snake, didn't you? This snake is a grey poupon color. There are stripes down either side made up of tiny dark spots. The crayfish snake is short and slender. The adult averages 18 to 30 inches in length. They are the diameter of the card-board rung of a pant coat hanger. I hope you can get a mental image because it took me a long time to come up with that comparison!

He is not called a crayfish snake because he scoots backwards when accosted! He prefers to dine upon crayfish that have just molted their skin. I forgot to put that term in the glossary so I'll say a little something here. All arthro-pods, i.e., insects, lobsters, spiders, crabs, and crayfish will shed their outer shell as they grow. For a short time just after they do this they are soft shelled and squashy. As a kid I fished for crawdads using a strip of bacon tied to the end of a string. I would occasionally catch what we called a "softy." Looking like a walking blob of Jello, they have to hide to avoid being eaten. The crayfish snake has a way of ferreting them out during this vulnerable time and downing them like a raw oyster!

That reminds me of an oyster joke. This salesman walked into a bar and sat down, see. At the end of the counter there was a little bowl containing a raw oyster. The sign behind it said: "TWENTY DOLLARS TO ANYONE WHO CAN SWALLOW THIS OYSTER AND KEEP IT DOWN." The salesman, a New Englander, called to the bar keep. "Are you serious about this oyster?" he asked. The bartender said, "You keep it down and here is your twenty!" The salesman grinned, picked up the bowl and quickly downed the marine morsel. The bartender watched and grinned. Then he said, "You know, you are the fifth person today to swallow that same oyster!" Where was I? Oh yea, crayfish snakes.

An interesting mating behavior occurs in these snakes. It seems almost romantic but after all, folks, these are snakes! The event takes place in the water at night. The female puts out her calling card in the form of the pheromone scent and draws several males. They intertwine forming a ball of snakes. This ball will float around all night. Only one copulation will take place during this ritual. Ain't nature grand!

The female gives birth to live young as do all the other water snakes.

This is a shy and nonaggressive water snake. His fellow water snakes could certainly take a lesson from him in the area of calm temperament. Because of his laid-back personality and being a total recluse he might be found in and around city park ponds and drainage ditches. He is similar to another crayfish snake, the Gulf crayfish snake. You will see this one before you might encounter the other.

The crayfish snake is a resident of East Texas all the way from the Panhandle to Brownsville.

Earth Snake

Talk about your dinky denizen! John Q. Citizen walked in the front door of the nature center with a snake of unbelievable size. He was all business and very serious as he related his story. It seems that this minuscule menace was being attacked by his dog. He fought off the dog and scooped up the snake in a coffee can. The man went on to say that the snake had an eye injury and might need some first aid.

First of all this snake was the diameter of a pencil lead and every bit of two inches long. It must have been a really petite-pawed poodle that could attack something of that size. Secondly, can a human being have better than 20-20 vision? This guy could see an eye injury? His dog had uncovered a newly hatched rough earth snake.

This snake will almost always be a dark, greyish brown. The tummy is an off white or as grandma likes to say "cream colored." There is no pattern and the young are the same color as the adults.

A real long rough earth snake is less than a foot long. He is about the diameter of a soda straw. Have you ever noticed that the people from the extreme north and over toward the east say "I think I'll have a soda" or "why don't you go to the store and get us some sodas." Down here we take soda for gas attacks or make a paste for a bee sting. I'm gettin' thirsty here so I think I'll have myself a big orange!

The rough earth snake is nonvenomous, nonaggressive, and its mouth is not big enough to bite people! His nose is shaped for burrowing through the soil in search of his favorite wormy meal. You might find him wiggling across the driveway at night. He will also fly toward your face in two or more pieces when you are edging the lawn and he gets caught in the blade. That is not an attack you understand!

There are quite a few similar snakes in Texas. They differ in color and the way their scales are arranged. If you have the need to know, well, get another book, and a life!

This is the most common snake in his range. He hails from anywhere in the eastern half of the state.

Flathead Snake

One of my former students brought a snake into my office for identification. I can do that so I carefully opened the plastic margarine tub and peeked inside. I picked up the small snake and proclaimed "this is a Plains blackhead snake, *Tantilla nigriceps,* that is just a little far from home." One of my colleagues looked at the snake and said "Dunlap, you either need longer arms or glasses, this snake has some sort of growth on its head!"

Feeling somewhat like a termite in a yo-yo I looked closer (or farther away) and discovered the amazing truth. Note: If you are just standing in the book store and reading this you'll notice that these words are designed to suck you into buying. If you have already purchased the book, well, gotcha! First of all, the snake was a flathead snake (good for this bit, don't you think?) and is one of our less common garden snakes in most of Texas. It was his dinner that got him into trouble. He had apparently discovered a roach egg case that had popped open to release the hatching insects. He must have waited patiently and simply gulped up each roach as it emerged from the case. Not wanting to leave any leftovers, he stuck his head in the case and became stuck! The roach egg case was a perfect, tight fit. Note: (yes, another one) Did you know that in deepest, darkest Africa where a bug called the Giant Hissing Cockroach is common, the natives eat them! I have read that if they are roasted properly they taste like avocado. Can you imagine a roach guacamole? I'd be afraid I'd get one of those little legs caught between my teeth. How do you floss a roach part?

This snake is one of those "ishes" of brown. The belly is pink. The head is sometimes a little darker than the rest of his body but don't count on it. All the identification guides say this snake has a head that is "flattened from top to bottom." That may be true if you caught him just right with the shovel!

This is another of your little bitty snakes. An adult will grow to ten inches. The babies are about three inches at hatching and the diameter of bailing wire.

He likes soft soil in which to dig. Your freshly turned flower bed makes a great place to hunt, sleep, make love, and do those things that snakes do. He eats soil-dwelling insect larvae and earthworms. He is nonvenomous and too small to bite you.

Just about all the Texas snakes that are solid colored and small could be mistaken for this critter. We have the rough earth snake, the ground snake, blackhead snake, just to name them all!

This snake is the most common serpent found in the eastern two thirds of Texas.

Garter Snake

Ask almost any nine-year-old kid about his encounter with a snake and he has a story to tell. Somewhere in his story he will mention a garter snake. It is the most common of the "common" names that we give unidentified snakes. There are really garter snakes almost all over Texas along with hundreds that we call garter snakes. These creatures are the most likely to be tolerated because they are most associated with the word "harmless."

My experience as a snake hunter places these snakes in the category of "snake most likely to bite me and hence become airborne!" I have yet to grab an escaping garter snake that it did not turn and implant its needle sharp, though very small, teeth in my hand.

The background color of all of our seven species of garter snake is dark. Some will have darker blotches, checks, or spots arranged within this dark background. The stripes are the thing. There will be one stripe down his back. The color of this stripe varies even among individuals of the same subspecies. There will be a stripe down each side. These stripes are not as showy colored as the top stripe.

Just to give you some idea of the size, all seven of our garter snakes adult-out at 15 to 30 inches. The diameter is somewhere between pointy finger and hot dog. They have a noticeable neck but don't panic with your "triangular shaped head, therefore it is poisonous" routine.

First of all, if you grab this snake, purely by accident I'm sure, he will musk all over you. Well, he may not get any on the soles of your feet but it's not because he didn't try! They do bite. Although they won't bite a nine-year-old and I'm not real sure why. They prefer to hang around wet places so watch around the pool, sauna, and any tall wet grass near the water hydrant. They dine on earthworms, frogs, toads, and an occasional salamander.

It is easy to relate the similar snakes. We are talking anything with stripes. There are ribbon snakes, patchnose snakes, and lined snakes, none of which are poisonous. They go by the attack name of "grass snakes."

At least one species of garter snake is found in every county in Texas.

Glossy Snake

All you Southern Texans may be interested in this snake. He might be mistaken for a copperhead on a bad day but he is nonvenomous and laid back.

The main color of this snake is a muckle-de-dung grey but he do shine like a new penny. He has dark brown saddle shaped designs down his back that are more or less equally spaced. Let us all call them blotches because that is what they are! They have white bellies.

The adult averages between 20 and 30 inches long and is about the diameter of a broom handle. They hunt at night and they find, kill, and devour lizards in their sleep. Did I make that sound sneaky and horrible? Snakes gotta do what snakes gotta do!

This is definitely a night traveler and can be seen crossing the road in the wee hours. Oh yes, have you heard this one? Why did the glossy snake cross the road? To show the armadillo that it could be done! (I am truly sorry about that one!) They love to burrow in sand and usually hide out there during the day. When surprised this snake will elevate the end of his tail and vibrate it wildly. He obviously does not know that people don't like rattlesnakes around here.

The look-alike list for this snake is extensive: bull snakes, prairie king snakes, Great Plains rat snakes and, if you use a little imagination, the Texas night snake.

I think I have already mentioned that he lives in South Texas and I don't lie!

Ground Snake

If I remember any of my history lessons, I seem to recall that Abe Lincoln wrote the Gettysburg Address on the back of an envelope while on a train en route to Gettysburg. I am sitting here in traffic and watching a train move back and forth in front of me for no apparent reason. It has been about five minutes and there is no escape. I'll make notes.

The ground snakes of Texas are the most varied in color of any snakes. My snake hunting buddies and I have been known to place small bets as to who could collect the greatest number of ground snakes of different colors. The engineer has gone to the bathroom. Taillights on the cars in front of me have started to change from brake to back-up colors. These are all snakes of the same species and inhabit the same environment. They are nonpoisonous and are not even capable of biting due to the size of their mouths. The train backed off the intersection. The cars are starting to go around the gates because the train did not back far enough to activate the raising of the gates. He noticed his mistake and slowly backed up another two feet. The gates raise and cars begin to move. The engineer is leaning on the window and watching the cars cross. As I watch the cars approach the crossing I see each driver slow, lean out the window, and make gestures that do not leave much to the imagination. The engineer just watches quietly as if to say "So, what's new?"

If you consult a stiff and usually dull reference book, you will find the COLOR section to be most of the information about the ground snake. I will narrow the color possibilities. Okay, think salmon colored bellies. I know that color is not on my color chart but use your imagination or ask your mother. Here is a partial list of colors: tan, brown, dull yellow, grey, orangeish, and some others that I don't have a name for. The backs can be striped, blotched, patched, spotted, solid, or pick one!

All of these colors are found on one species of snake. The size is the same. None are usually over one foot long. They are slim for their length and about the diameter of your pinky finger.

If for no other reason, you should tolerate them because of their food habits. They eat centipedes, scorpions, and spiders. They live with us and around us. If you have stacks and piles of things around the yard, then you have set up housekeeping for these animals. If you have a vacant lot next door, be sure to bug the real estate people about keeping it mowed and clean. Threaten to sue if you are attacked and wrestled to the ground by a ferocious ground snake!

Unless you are into counting scales on snakes, you can't tell the difference between these and most other small snakes. We have flathead snakes, earth snakes, and black-head snakes and things can get confusing. These snakes do not bite humans. If your relatives have you classified any differently, just be cool!

These variable colored snakes can be found everywhere in Texas except in the east.

Hognose Snake

Please let me introduce, and will you please make welcome, the darndest snake you will ever meet. These harmless snakes have caused more trauma and cleaning bills than any other serpent. If you have always wanted a unique pet and your "pet rock" is getting old, the hognose snake is the critter for you.

It was a dark and stormy night (man, I love that intro!). The night air was a little cool so you thought you might get a fire going in the old fireplace. You need wood so you travel to that cord of oak that has been stacked beside the garage for two or three years and is beginning to rot. (There is really no need for a fireplace in Texas!) There are two stray logs on the driveway that have become separated from the rest of the stack. You are one to take the easy way out so you bend and pick these up. Some motion is evident out of the corner of your eye. SNAKE! He has coiled. His head and body are flattened and he is prepared to strike. You weren't really sure that cobras were found in this part of the world. Maybe up in Oklahoma but not here. Whack! You drop the oak on the snake. All is quiet. Using the 20 foot extension pole on your telescoping pool scooper you slowly turn the log over. There he is and he is dead! You are one smart cookie and you recognize the symptoms. He is on his back. His mouth is open and his tongue is hanging out. You have killed the famous "spreadin' adder."

You have bought this book and you need to see his back to determine color so you use a shorter stick to roll him over. Suddenly he rolls back over! He was playing "possum!"

The hognose snake is the only one in Texas with a cute little turned up nose. The patchnosed snake has a patch and it is not cute nor is it turned up. There are three species and they all have the same nose. The colors will drive you crazy.

Here is a partial list of main colors and you can add "ishes" to both sides of each of them: yellow, brown, grey, olive, orange, red and black. They all have an unpatterned greyish belly and that is what you will see second! The pattern, when you can see one, will start with a dark blotch on either side of his head and the rest of his body can be best described as "spotty-checked."

Our Texas hognoses range from 15 to 30 inches long. They have relatively stout bodies (think of a relative that the family refers to as "stout") for their length.

The hognose seems to like areas near bodies of water. Tall grass and forest floor litter are his best hiding and hunting places. This snake is one of the few of nature's creatures that makes it a point to eat toads. He will devour a frog on occasion and the baby snakes will eat insects and worms. There have been reports of them eating dead stuff. I have fed them dead toads in captivity, and they seem to enjoy not having to put up a fight.

Besides the other species of hognose, the only snakes that are similar would be the copperheads. The only similarity there is in the area of color. A closer look will help you decide the difference. If you can't tell the difference between a hognose snake and a copperhead, then you should not spend time looking any closer!

At least one of our three species of hognose may be found in every county in Texas.

Indigo Snake

It was years ago. The caller informed me that she must find a home for her pet snake because she had gotten married and had quit her job. I told her to "come on down!" She bumped and ground (grinded?) through the door. She did a "bump and grind" through the door. Does that sound better? The staff hopped to attention! She was obviously a former stripper with her clothes on! She donated a big, beautiful indigo snake to the collection and I have not seen nor heard from her since. Honest!

This snake is the way I once liked my steaks. He is big and rare! He is the biggest snake in Texas but perhaps not the rarest. It depends on who you ask.

This is a very dark snake that literally glows in the dark. The belly shows hints of orange hidden in a deep blue-black. If you notice a pattern it is most likely just a product of your imagination.

There are reliable records of Texas indigo snakes growing to a length of eight and one-half feet. They are about the diameter of a Texsun orange juice can. If the truth be known, that is really grapefruit juice in the can and was put there in an effort to get rid of an excess of that foul tasting grapefruit juice! Where was I? Oh yes, the males get a little longer than the females.

Ask any snake collector that has ever tried to maintain this snake and he will most likely compare him to having a myna bird. This snake is a very smelly creature that will both musk and spread feces at the opening of a door or the dropping of a hat. They are so totally terrestrial that just lifting them off the ground sends them into a real frenzy. They will bite and have rather large sharp teeth that really make a point. They never seem to get used to being handled and want no part of human contact.

They dine upon small mammals, birds, lizards and even other snakes. He is most definitely a South Texas snake, and I have neither seen nor heard about one in years. Have I distanced myself far enough from the stripper?

King Snake, Grey-banded

This gentle animal is the jewel of the collection. Mention the name to anyone in Texas who loves or even likes snakes, and his eyes will light up. I doubt seriously if you will ever encounter one other than in the zoo, but when you do, you will always remember it. They are so colorful, you'd think they must be put together by a committee at Walt Disney Studios. I have even known snake haters to say something remarkable like, "I wouldn't hurt that snake — he's too pretty!"

As the name implies, this animal is a beautiful silvery grey, with dark black cross bands. Right behind his head, there might be a black patch that encircles another bright orange patch. The snake's color is highly variable. For example, I have described the alterna phase and then the Blair phase, which may consist of a snake with grey, white, black, and orange bands, or the dark Blair phase, which consists of black, white, and dark grey bands. In any event, you will recognize him when you see him.

The adult grey-banded king snake averages thirty inches in length. He is relatively thin.

This animal is a night feeder and prefers to dine upon nesting rodents or sleeping lizards which are located by scent. The most common place you will encounter one of these snakes would be in the pet shop, because just recently, a fail-safe method of reproducing them in captivity has produced a large number of them for pet sales.

If you use your imagination just a little, you could compare this snake with the poisonous Texas coral snake, or the harmless milk snake. Those snakes are much more slender and their heads are round as opposed to the triangular shaped head of the king snake.

This snake, in all its radiant glory, makes its home in areas from El Paso down through the Big Bend region.

King Snake, Prairie

I am sure I will edit this out later, but as I sit here at the keyboard I have some thoughts about nonfiction writing. I just picked up one of those "wildlife" cards that tells you everything you need to know about a particular animal. Well I just happened to be reading about the barn owl. All went well until I came to the heading LIFESPAN: and it said two years. I have a barn owl in my collection, and he is appropriately named "Barney." I got old Barney in 1985. He is still alive and well and eating three mice every day! As I sit here he is a ripe old eight-year-old! The only reliable nonfiction seems to be from only those writers that have the experience. Or, if you believe everything you read, you should not read!

Keeping that in mind, I will discuss the prairie king snake. This snake is the ho-hum snake of the collector's world. It seems that all his relatives are much prettier than he. You'll have to look in someone else's book with big color photos but check out the scarlet king snake, the grey-banded king snake, and the speckled king snake. They are really handsome.

I can testify to the fact that prairie king snakes are the kings of escape technique. Here comes the story, so if you bore easily, you might go to the fridge for a beverage while I relate. One of the most important pieces of equipment to a snake hunter is the snake bag. These bags can be custom made with monogrammed hems or the low rent type which are simply pillow cases. My financial status dictates the pillow case. I always carry three or four into the field. I put empty margarine containers and coffee cans in one pillow case for housing smaller critters. These all dangle from the back of the belt which leaves the hands free to flip boards and handle the snake stick as you traipse through the countryside.

On one such hunting adventure I turned over a large piece of plywood and there he was! He was one large prairie king snake. Stop here and realize the feeling. You throw the basketball at the hoop and it goes in. You buy a beverage and the machine gives you more change than you put in. Drawing to an inside straight. You get my drift. I bagged the snake and tied the knot in the top just like I had done a thousand times before and slipped the snake-in-the-bag under my belt in the back. I continued down the slope. I had walked only a few yards when I felt a tickle on my bare back about even with my shoulder blades. I reached around and guess what! The snake had unthreaded the knot and was on his way to my shirt collar!

This is one of those dark shades of color snakes. The main color may be grey, dark olive, deep brown, or almost black. The pattern consists of even darker blotches down the back. The belly is rather striking (I heard that at a fashion show!) with its squarish blotches on a white background.

Note: If you sneak into the fridge and take a slug of milk straight from the carton, you might use the same secrecy to perform this operation. The easiest way to separate those paper coffee filters is to put the edge of the one you suspect as being two between your lips and simply open your mouth. I'm still working on separating the edges of those plastic trash bags!

The prairie king snake grows to a length of three feet. The average snake is a little over two feet. He is about the diameter of a three iron golf club grip.

This snake is secretive and usually only comes out from under the rocks, grass clumps, or mammal burrows at night. He is a handleable snake and usually just vibrates his tail a bit when grabbed. Although the snake prefers warm-blooded prey such as mice, rats, birds, and baby rabbits, he has been known to consume frogs, toads, and other snakes. He is a powerful constrictor.

There is a prairie king snake "look-alike" in the Great Plains rat snake. I could say that the colors are lighter in the rat snake, but what are your chances of having both of them together at the same time? They are also alike in temperament and behavior so not to worry.

The prairie king snake makes his home everywhere we consider East Texas. He can also be found in the northernmost rectangle of the Panhandle.

King Snake, Speckled

This is not a snake you would invite over for a family gathering if you happen to be another snake. The king snake clan members are well known for eating their relatives!

This king snake is your basic black with yellow or gold specks (hence the name "speckled"). We all know that opinions are like noses in that everybody has one, so if you see a dark chocolate brown snake with specks, it's probably the same one. The quick glance you will probably get may not be enough to see any form in these specks. However, the pattern does vary between two different species that occur in Texas. Not to worry, it's still basically the same snake.

The specks on our most common speckled king snake are seemingly equidistant from each other and form no noticeable pattern. You may hear the common name chain king snake, and that refers to the Florida king snake. Our local variety is sometimes called the salt and pepper king snake. I never cared much for that common name because I would be leery of salt that was a shade of yellow!

The part of the snake that you probably saw would have been about the diameter of a broom handle. That was an adult and the young are, of course, uh, smaller. The average adult measures about a yardstick. They have been reported as growing to six feet but that is not common. Even at that length they are not very tall.

I want to talk about his lifestyle, but I always want to say "Of the Rich and Famous" when I hear that word. I watch too much television. What were we talking about? Oh yeah, snakes. The speckled king snake is a forest dwelling creature and also likes grassy, damp pastures. He will hide under just about anything. You are more likely to see one of these crawling across a pile of dead leaves in a city park than across your driveway.

You might be digging in your flower bed in the spring and come across a batch of white, oblong, squashy eggs under about three inches of soil. This snake usually lays eggs in the soft soil beneath the leaf litter in the forest. If you find these eggs, you can just leave them alone (preferable) or call the zoo and someone there will tell you to leave them alone! What I am saying here is "leave them alone!" They are not poisonous or dangerous. The snakes aren't either.

These snakes are powerful constrictors. They eat mostly small mammals such as rats, mice, and (despicable aren't they?) baby rabbits. We already know about his cannibalistic tendencies.

I have already mentioned the Florida king snake which has specks in a chain pattern across his back. The desert king snake is also black and yellow but there is so much yellow that the black takes on the appearance of patches.

Oh yes, I should mention another rather obnoxious habit. Grabber beware! These snakes have musk glands at the rear end. When they are grabbed, handled roughly, or immobilized in any way the snake will let go a foul smelling mucus that stinks to high heaven. This survival technique is logical if you stop and think. If you bit into your hamburger and it took a dump on you, wouldn't you spit it out?

The speckled king snake is found in the upper coastal region and to the east and north all the way to the Panhandle.

Lined Snake

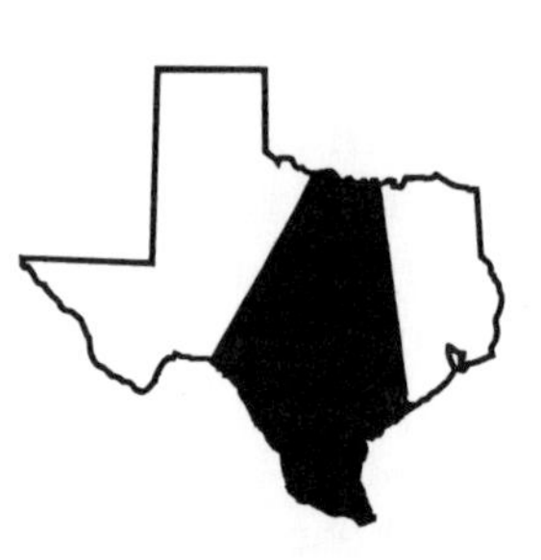

Once upon a time, in a land far, far away...actually in a land right outside your back door, there lived a little striped snake.

Near the end of the fall season I spend a lot of time trying to convince my wife that the leaves in the driveway are part of my compost pile. She lets that go on until the last football game on television and then I am forced to pick up those leaves. The only reward I get is that I never know what has decided to take up residence in the decaying leaf pile. Along with the slugs, snails, pillbugs, and earthworms, I find at least one lined snake. As a kid I thought that this snake only existed in a tight coil like a fire hose. The first time I saw one crawling I was surprised. I was a real dumb kid.

This is one of those snakes that is most identifiable from the belly side up. There are two rows of half-moon-shaped dark spots running the length of the belly. He has a stripe down his back that could be just about any color. You might see white, yellow, orange, or light grey. There is a stripe down each side of the snake and these also vary in color.

The much-too-serious reference books mention a lot of lengths but I can safely say between 8 and 15 inches. I guess I have led a sheltered snake hunting life because I have never seen one that was over 10 inches long. The diameter is about that of a good milkshake straw.

These snakes really dig earthworms. I mean they don't actually dig up earthworms. I mean they really like to eat earthworms. You know what I mean! They are not poisonous and do not bite humans. If you bug them, they might flatten their bodies and give you a couple of quick fake strikes. They were once very common in every backyard within their range. The use of pesticides and fertilizers have drastically reduced their numbers in and around human abodes. You might still flip one up with the edger blade on occasion.

The central lined and the Texas lined snake are the only ones that are similar. From a distance the garter and ribbon snake kinda remind you of a lined snake. I assume you have met many of them before.

Our two species of lined snake inhabit the center third of the state from the Red River to the Rio Grande.

Longnose Snake

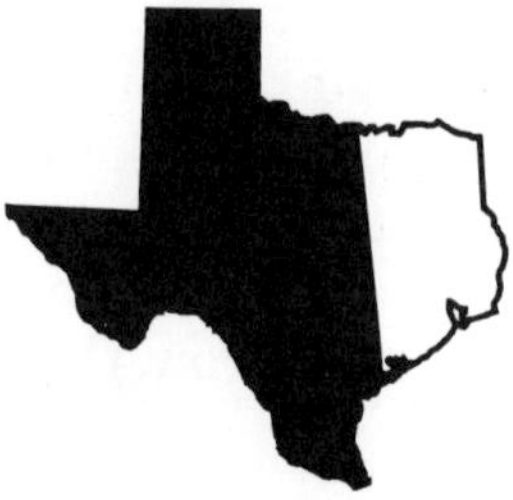

Don't expect Jimmy Durante here but this snake has a long nose as compared to other snakes. If you are a snake collector, this would be a jewel in your inventory because of its bright colors.

Speaking of colors, we will do that now to give me time to remember a story because right off the bat I can't think of one! He is a bright red, black, and yellow snake. The color pigment is scattered so as to give the appearance of being speckled. There is a strong design that looks like hourglass cross bands over his back. If you get down face to face, his long nose might have an upturned look. It will not be to the degree we see in the hognose snake or a department store clothes model.

This snake grows to a length of 16 to 30 inches and is the diameter of the cardboard crossbar of a pants coat hanger (I liked that one!). He burrows most of the time and enjoys lizards as a main meal.

You are in luck, I remember a story. "Hello, is this Mr. Dunlap?" I love talking on the phone so I replied, "That depends. Do you want something?" Chuckle, chuckle and on with it. "Mr. Dunlap, my pet snake bleeds on my hand almost every time I pick him up. I can't find any injuries anywhere on him and I don't drink!" I wanted to suggest that he just quit picking him up but I remained cool. After a few hundred questions I realized that this man was just provoking the defense strategy of the Texas longnose snake. When molested this snake will writhe violently while defecating all over himself and the offending hand. The liquid part of the feces is tinged with blood.

The longnose is at home in the western two-thirds of the state.

Milk Snake

From what I read I am to assume that the milk snake got its name from an old belief that this snake could actually milk a cow. I've tried to milk a cow and believe me it is no picnic! It takes skilled hands and concentration. All this snake has is a small mouth full of needle sharp little teeth, no hands, and no known taste for milk. These snakes are often found in barns and around feed troughs because that is where the mice hang out.

The milk snake is our most common coral snake mimic. It causes scouts to burst into verse. "Red and yellow, kill a fellow. Red and black, friend of Jack." You may want to memorize this poem and have a copy in your backpack for future reference. The poem refers to the arrangement of the red, yellow, and black bands of color that surround the snake. The red and yellow bands join together on the coral snake and the red and black bands touch on the harmless milk snake. These bands on the milk snake stop at the bottom edges where the pale colored belly scales begin. The rings on the poisonous coral snake go all the way around.

The average length of the milk snake is between 15 and 32 inches. The milk snake is bigger around than the coral snake. If your imagination is on fast forward, just think of the cardboard part of a pants coat hanger. I liked that analogy the last time I used it also.

This is a secretive snake and you might encounter it under piles of junk in the backyard after it has avoided being cleaned up for a few years. It does not exhibit much family pride in that it will eat most of its own family if it gets the chance! It also likes to eat barnyard mice and a baby chick or two.

There are four different kinds of milk snake that you might find here in Texas. They all are very similar in appearance and they are all harmless. They are not prone to bite unless you cause them physical pain. They all in turn look something like the Texas longnose snake. The longnose snake has red saddle shaped patches that might be mistaken for stripes if noticed over the shoulder as you depart there running.

Of the four milk snakes found in Texas we have at least one species found in every nook and cranny. Does the word "habitat" sound better?

Mud Snake

This is commonly referred to as the western mud snake and is found in East Texas. That is because East Texas is the western extent of his range. I think I might get a headache if I think about this too much so I will press on.

The mud snake has a hysterical, historical background that will amuse and amaze you. Maybe it won't but who knows! When handled this snake will wrap around parts of your anatomy and press the tip of its tail against your skin. The last scale on the tail tip forms a little sharp spur. This was once thought to be a stinger that could deliver a fatal sting. Furthermore, this snake has a habit of lying around in a circular coil. This added to the story that this snake could grab its tail in its mouth and "roll down" a man and sting him to death. It is believed that sometimes the snake will miss and hit a bush or tree. The venom is strong enough to kill the tree! Ain't that a hoot!

The mud snake is your basic glossy black. The belly is a beautiful red and black checked pattern. The back is patternless. The adults are known to grow to over six feet long. The average mud snake gets about a yardstick long and the diameter of a broom handle.

The mud snake, as his name implies, likes muddy places. He might be found when you drag a log up from the lake edge so you can sit down to watch your cork or perhaps to just remove your cork. He has a very specific diet and will usually only eat weird amphibians. He dines upon eels, sirens, and amphiumas. Those last two look a lot like eels.

Unless you have a vivid imagination or just don't really care, this snake does not have a look-alike in Texas. I could tell you why it does not look like a water moccasin, but if you think all snakes found near water are poisonous, why bother!

The mud snake might be found in the eastern fourth of the state.

Patchnose Snake

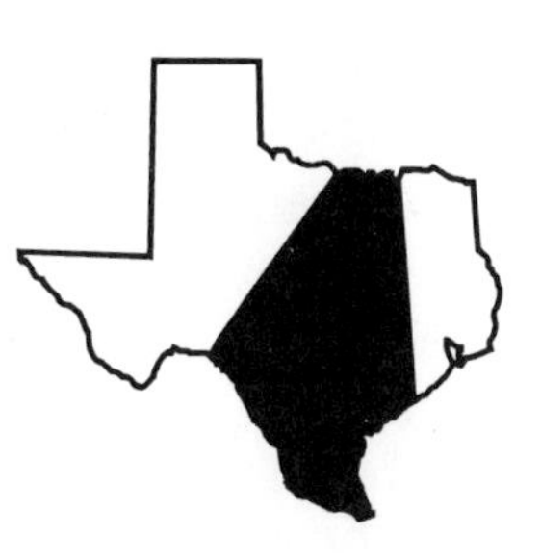

The name might make you think of the patch on the knee of your kids' blue jeans. That's not it. Think of the last time you wrapped a gift. After folding the ends you are left with a pointy fold that comes out in the center of the end. Are you following me here? Some people fold the point so that it comes up even with the edge of the package. If you didn't do that, and just folded the point around the end of the package, that point looks like the nose on a patchnose snake! I went a long way for that one!

This is yet another of the striped snakes in Texas. This one is basic black with yellow or tan stripes. There are two other species that are less common that are light grey with dark stripes.

The adult patchnose snake averages between 20 and 36 inches. He would be thin for his length.

In captivity the patchnose eats mostly lizards and will take a smaller snake, mouse, or frog. He also seems to like reptile eggs. He may use that wierd proboscis to root them out of the dirt. He likes to spend time under things and will not be found unless you use your wierd appendages to move logs and rocks around in the woods.

He hunts during the day and may appear as a streak when he slithers out through the grass at an alarming rate of speed. If picked up, he will flail vigorously and might even nip once. He will then go for your throat, bite, and you will be dead in two minutes! Just kidding. I wanted to make sure you were still paying attention.

The Texas patchnose snake can be found in the central region of the state from Brownsville almost to the Red River. His look-alikes, the mountain patchnose snake and the Big Bend patchnose, are both found in the Big Bend area of Texas.

Racer

My grandmother always had the greatest farm snake stories, and she could scare the beejeebees out of me in a minute. One of her best was being chased by snakes. She would always squat to talk to me. She would not bend or stand or sit. She would squat. She was the only relative who would call me by my first and middle name. Her kids all had names that went together like Billy Joe, Johnnie Gene, Bobby Ray, and eight others.

"Jimmy Doyle, come here, I want to tell you about a snake I saw today." This one was during one of her daily trips to the barn to feed chickens or slop hogs. The barn was about a quarter mile through the pasture and was a trip I had made many times. I don't ever remember a snake encounter but I do remember stepping over things like cow patties, horn toads, and goat-head stickers.

Once upon a time in a land far away... That's not it! Granny said she was carrying the five-gallon slop bucket and just sauntering along when she noticed something sticking up above the Johnson grass. She stopped and looked and to her horror (she did not like snakes!) it was a snake! After general panic she turned slowly and started walking back toward the house. The snake began to follow! His head was sticking out a foot above the top of the grass. She walked faster, the snake slithered faster. The bucket went down, the snake came on. Granny broke into a trot and the snake lost no ground. I giggle here because Granny was only four feet tall, both ways! She said she hit the back porch on the fly and she lost track of the snake a hundred yards or so before. By the time she got her gun and stepped back out on the porch the snake was nowhere in sight. "What kind of snake was it, Granny?" "Well, Jimmy Doyle, it must have been a racer because they are the fastest and meanest snakes around here!" I became a grass watcher for a long time after that.

My theory, and I know you are on the edge of your seat for this, is that when John Q. Human and slithery snake first see each other they both have immediate flight in mind. They both take off — in the same direction. Hence we have, "That snake chased me all the way back to the house!"

From all I know and have read and heard, there are no snakes in Texas that chase people. Don't believe anything you hear and only half of what you see.

The racer is fast. I can testify because I have chased many of them for collecting. Consider these colors in a blur! The babies are brightly colored and very strongly patterned. They lose this brilliance and pattern as they get older. The most common racer in Texas is the yellow-bellied racer. He is a solid color that ranges from a dark olive green to a greenish blue. The adult reaches 30 to 54 inches in length and is the diameter of a broom handle. They are aggressive snakes and will bite at the drop of a hat or when grabbed.

Racers love insects such as grasshoppers, crickets, and cicadas — ah!, story here! I was snake hunting and walking down a back country dirt road. I noticed some movement near the grass at road's edge, so I went into my crouch and began to sneak forward. Here is the scene. A young racer had attacked a cicada. If you call them locusts you are wrong! Anyway, this small snake had grabbed the large cicada by the head. The cicada wings were unencumbered and operating frantically. With each flurry of attempted flight the forward portion of the snake would be lifted off the ground a few inches. Neat fight! The snake won and the wings stopped when they were halted by encroaching snake lips!

About the only snakes that are similar to the racers are other racers. The coachwhips are bigger and of a different color.

The yellow-bellied racer is found throughout most of Texas. They are sparse or nonexistant in extreme west and east Texas. There are five other species of racer known to occur in the state. Just in case it comes up at a party they are: Mexican racer, southern black racer, buttermilk racer, tan racer, and the Central American speckled racer. I would not want you to appear uninformed.

Rat Snake, Great Plains

If you are attending a garden party hosted by your local herpetologist, you might hear this snake referred to as an Emory's rat snake. That is the subspecies name and it was first described by somebody named Emory. I am quite sure you needed that bit of information.

Well, what can I say. This is a pretty snake. But, you don't like snakes, am I correct? This is the snake that I enjoy using for classroom presentations because they are not prone to bite.

The Great Plains rat snake has a light grey background with grey-brown blotches all down his back. It can also be said that he has a diamond on his head, or at least that is the design.

You might consider this to be a big snake because the adult might be about three feet long. He is about the diameter of a hoe handle.

He squeezes his food. He eats mostly small rodents as well as ground nesting birds, frogs, and lizards. This is one of the few snakes that doesn't seem to have any taste for his own kind.

This is most definitely an after hours serpent. He waits until well after dark before he emerges from under the logs, boards, or pieces of sheetrock where he spends the day.

The prairie king snake is the spittin' image of this snake. The colors are just slightly different but the personality is about the same.

The Great Plains rat snake is found all over the state of Texas. Well, if you live in Texarkana, you might never see one but don't let it keep you up nights.

Rat Snake, Texas

Read my lips, "R-A-T snake!" I am not saying "R-A-T-T-L-E-S-N-A-K-E!" Out in the rural areas these are called chicken snakes. They get that name because they do like to spend a lot of time hanging around the ol' henhouse. They eat rats and mice which also hang around the ol' henhouse eating the chicken feed and so it goes.

As a kid it was one of my chores to gather eggs in the henhouse every morning. My grandmother would give me a little tin pail and send me off through the pasture to the building which was about 200 yards away. I remember having to dodge cow patties, goat-head stickers, horned toads, and roofing nails just to get down there. The rows of nest boxes were waist high to a grown person which put them just above eye level for me. I would move from box to box blindly burrowing under startled hens to remove the fruits of their labor. For your information, rat snakes not only eat chickens but they will dine on an available egg. (* Look for an interesting and slightly humorous anecdote at the end of this piece.) On more than one occasion my hand would fall upon the coiled body of a rat snake. The snake not only had come for dinner but was enjoying the 100 degree F that a sitting hen can produce. I learned early that snakes had to make a living too so I would just skip that box. The one time I mentioned it to my grandmother was a mistake. She ran from the kitchen to the tool shed. She armed herself with a hoe and then attacked the hen house with great gusto. With a quick flip she removed the squawking chicken. Another move and the snake was out of the box and on the ground. Chop chop, dead snake! My grandmother didn't like snakes. She would then declare the area off-limits because she was convinced that a snake would not die until the sun went down.

If you chance to see this snake in the slither mode and get a glimpse of his undulating stretched skin you will see that it is red between the scales. The belly is an off-white with dark squares. Unless he is hanging from a tree or squashed on the road I do not think you will see his belly. His bulk is almost black with a tiny fleck of yellow here and there.

This snake is so dark that it is difficult to see the diamond-shaped patchy pattern. The babies are strongly marked with brown patches on a grey background, but the design fades with age. Other things fade with age, even in snakes!

The adults average just over a yard but the record is a little over seven feet. He is about the circumference of a hoe handle. That is a bit slim for his length. He loves to climb and is one of the few Texas snakes likely to be found high in trees, hidden in attics, or occasionally wrapped around the engine block of your Toyota. He prefers to dine upon poikilothermic animals (the glossary is in the back someplace) such as birds, rodents, and other small mammals.

If bird eggs are all that stick around after he is noticed he might consume a couple. My good 'ol Grandaddy (here it comes!) used to tell me it was easy to catch a "chicken snake" which is another common name for the rat snake. You just build a box and cut a one-inch diameter hole in one side. Actually Grandaddy would just make a circle with his fingers and say "'bout that big." He wasn't much on math. Inside this box you would place two or three hen eggs. Put the box in the henhouse and wait. The theory was that the snake would crawl into the box, swallow the eggs, and the egg, being larger than the hole, would prevent the snake from crawling out of the box. I personally never tried it because I was still suffering the embarrassment from a previous story. I asked him how I might catch a bird. He told me to sneak up behind the bird and pour salt on its tail. After a few tries, being a highly intelligent four-year-old, I deduced that you could not get close enough because the bird would fly away. Grandaddy was ready. He said all you have to do is put your baseball cap on backwards. The bird could then be approached because he would think you were going the other way!

This snake would not be guilty of giving your dog or cat a run for their money. If the prey is too large to be swallowed quickly or if it resists too vigorously, it will first be squeezed with a couple of body loops. The then suffocated entree would be swallowed whole.

The Texas rat snake is found from central Texas to the east from border to border.

* I always watched my grandmother cook breakfast. She would crack the egg into a small bowl before she dumped it into the hot bacon grease for frying. I always wanted to ask her the reason until one morning the question answered itself. She took one of the eggs I had gathered and cracked it into the bowl. What came out was either most of a baby chick or a raw oyster that had found its way into a chicken egg!

Rat Snake, Trans-Pecos

I think this snake is the most beautiful of the Texas snakes. You snake haters might beg to disagree. I really like his "popeyed" face. The eyes are big and round and seem to be misplaced. There are no other snakes that have these eyes.

The main color here is a yellow green. The second color would be black or really dark brown. I have heard this animal called the "H Snake." He has H-shaped markings on his back which form two dark stripes that extend from stem to stern. There is no pattern in the yellow-green main color.

These snakes average about a yardstick long and are slim for their length. They are so wimpy that they will not bite even when snatched from under a cactus plant. The Trans-Pecos rat snake dines upon smaller animals which include both mammals and reptiles. He is not known to devour other snakes.

The Trans-Pecos rat snake likes to crawl around beneath the surface through mammal burrows or cracks and crevices. He comes up top at night and those big round eyes help him locate prey by sight.

I am happy to say that there is not another snake living in Texas that looks like this one. He makes his home in far West Texas from El Paso south through the Big Bend region.

Ribbon Snake

Ah yes, the long thin ribbon snake with the spot on top of his head. This spot is really the identifying characteristic of the ribbon snake. It is as memorable as the white spot you find on that little black furry spider you see walking along on the drapes. I am fishing for fodder here because for the life of me I can't think of much to say about this snake. I do smile when I have just fed one of my captive ribbon snakes and he has a very noticeable, unsightly lump in his body. I do marvel at the fact that it takes this Berol #2 pencil thin snake a long time to kill and swallow a big meal. If it is handled too soon thereafter, it can regurgitate said meal in a matter of a few seconds. I became painfully aware of that phenomenon after bagging one and letting the bag bounce under the back of my belt on my butt for half a day. He heaved right away and I noticed the smell and felt the wet (arg!) bag against my jeans at about the same time.

This is another basic striped snake. The main color is a dark green sometimes with a bluish tint. There are three stripes. The one down the back is usually yellow. The side stripes are lighter in color.

It may be found in or near bodies of water throughout about three fourths of the state. It will eat anything that lives in or near the water that moves and is the right size. They range in length from 20 to 34 inches and as I have said they are thin. An adult that is over twenty-five inches long weighs only 6 ounces.

All striped snakes are similar. If you make a mistake in your identification, not to worry. None of the Texas striped snakes are poisonous. They all will bite you if you pick them up and they will continue to bite until you release your hold.

There are four species of ribbon snakes in Texas. Their combined geographical range just about covers the whole state. I just know you are sitting on the edge of your chair for me to name them so I will. Relax for a moment. They are: the western ribbon snake, the redstripe ribbon snake, the Gulf Coast ribbon snake and, last but by no means least, the arid land ribbon snake. That last one sounds like somebody ran out of snake names!

Ringneck Snake

My world renowned and most talked about ringneck snake encounter will be first here (I don't believe any of that stuff either!). He is little and picked on by every predator in the world. But he has a gimmick. In nature you will survive if you have a gimmick. I was deep in the woods with snake stick in hand and having a great time. I had just bagged two rough earth snakes and a baby speckled king snake so things were lookin' good. I pulled back a piece of tin and there he lay. He saw me and went into his act. The end of his tail curled up and twisted upside down. The underside of his body is a bright orange so the curl was very obvious. You see, when this snake does this act in the presence of a bird it attracts the peck at the tail. The snake does not die from a head wound. Ain't that cute? This snake must taste really bad because there is usually only one strike and the predator moves along for something tastier.

This is a dark slate grey snake with a golden ring around its neck. The belly is yellow and turns a bright orange-red as you get closer to the tail. You will also notice some little half-moon spots located randomly along the belly.

Here again we have a dinky denizen of the dirt. The adults measure from 10 to 14 inches and are the diameter of a soda straw. They do not bite humans but they do have a slightly toxic saliva for use in subduing their food. They eat earthworms, salamanders, and an occasional frog.

These snakes are the kings of the homebodies. A group marked by science persons for field studies spent their lives in an area that measured no more than 400 feet in diameter. If they left, it was for a reason. When the season changed they might travel to a hibernation site. I have an uncle who drives to Miami every winter. Another reason to roam is to a summer egg-laying site. I have another uncle and we will leave it there!

The ringneck is similar to the other two species of ringneck known to occur in Texas and that makes sense. The very young brown snake could be mistaken for a ringneck from a distance.

The Missipi, prairie, and regal ringnecks occupy about all of the state except for the Valley.

Tree Snake

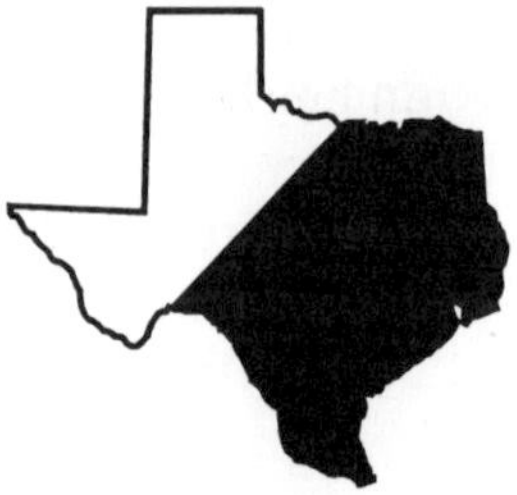

He is commonly called a "grass snake" because he is green. Actually, he spends all of his time in the trees trying to look like a twig so a big, hungry, and sometimes early bird doesn't make him a meal!

There are a lot of very descriptive adjectives for the color green. We have emerald, leaf, Kelly, grass, signal light, money, bright, and dark green just to name a few. Well, this snake is just green and you can choose your own adjective. Don't look for a pattern because there is none. The lips, chin, and belly are yellow.

The tree snake is long and thin (the better to resemble twigs with my dear!). The adults grow to between 20 and 30 inches and are the diameter of a pencil.

The tree snake dines on insects such as grasshoppers, crickets, caterpillars, and an arachnid or two such as spiders and scorpions. It is a slow-moving, easy-to-grab snake. It doesn't bite humans. The camouflage is complete. When this snake senses danger it will respond by freezing in place. It will even sway with the breeze to complete the deception. It seems to prefer the dense growth of vegetation along or near any body of water.

There are two species that might pop up in Texas. Both of them look alike so don't let it bother you. Here is a small insignificant note. The bright green will not remain on a dead snake. A dead tree snake will change color to a very ugly, Christmas tie blue.

The most common species of tree snake in Texas is called the rough green snake. He can be found in most of the state except for the far west and the Panhandle. You couldn't even begin to guess what the other one is called. Give up? It is called the western smooth green snake. I'm not making that up! He makes his home a little north of Houston on the coast and in one county in the Panhandle. That was a family started when a weird uncle green snake hitched a pickup ride up north!

Water Snake, Blotched

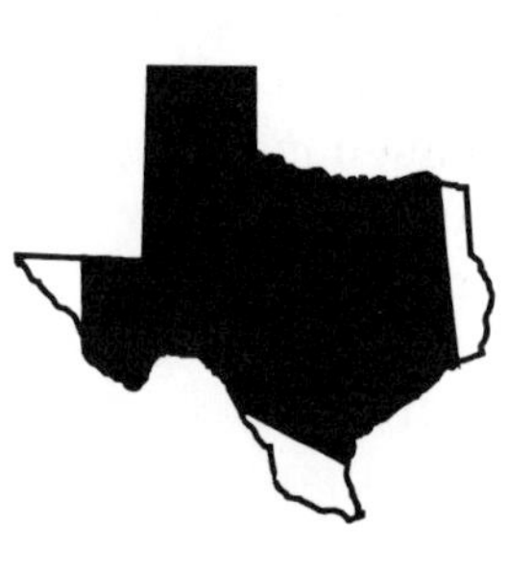

This snake looks a lot like the diamondback water snake that I described somewhere else in this book. The main difference is the colors are darker and the disposition is a little different — that being he is a little less aggressive. Beware of grabbing him because he will still hang a fang in you!

The main color is a dark, muckle-de-dung green with slightly noticeable thin black bands that cross his back. You may notice some light or white wide lines between the black. If you see this much, you might also notice some blood and a stray gut or two. He would most likely be dead! I would love to do another paragraph here, but that's about it on color!

Size-wise, this is a repeat of the other water snakes in that he is usually two to three feet in length. This snake doesn't get any bigger around than the rest of them!

This water snake, like the others, eats mostly fish, frogs, tadpoles, and occasionally crawfish when he needs his teeth cleaned! The chocolate-brown babies like shallow water and the adults go for the rocky outcroppings along the stream bed channels. This snake likes to travel at night, especially after heavy rains that wash insects out of the trees and bring out the frogs and toads.

I once watched a blotched water snake attack a bullfrog by grabbing him by the front leg. The bullfrog was very large and very strong and upset by having a snake hanging off his foot. He decided to leave, and using his long, muscular rear legs he jumped straight up. The water snake, being much smaller, had no choice but to follow along! They both disappeared from sight, the bullfrog definitely in charge of the situation!

The blotched water snake is actually the closest in appearance to the water moccasin. The distinguishing characteristics should be viewed only on a dead snake. The reason is, you can't see pinhead-sized facial pits or elliptical pupils of the poisonous water moccasin from across the creek! The blotched water snake is also longer and thinner in body configuration than is the water moccasin.

The blotched water snake is found just about everywhere in Texas, except for extreme east, extreme south, or extreme west. That leaves a lot if you really think about it!

Water Snake, Broad-banded

A water snake is a water snake is a water snake. I will mention at least four of the most common species found in Texas because I would hate to invoke the wrath of the "Water Snake Lovers of America," nor would I care to infuriate some high-paid government bureaucrat who has a grant to study "Minnow Length Preference of the Rare Harter's Water Snake." Actually, these species vary so widely in color and distribution that I would not want to encounter one that I forgot to write about!

The main color of the broad-banded water snake is a dark black with bright yellow or orange cross bands. The pattern could be defined as wide, irregular bands — the most noticeable colors being yellow and black with lighter orange in patches along the sides. They have a dappled yellow belly marked with large brown patches.

The adults average about two feet long and about the diameter of a fifty-cent piece. This is another one of those water snakes that is beaten, shot at, run from, and generally despised because it is thought to be a ferocious water moccasin. This snake prefers to spend its day on a partially submerged log or hiding in a "snake hole" in the bank side. He prefers hunting and making love at night!!

As I said in the beginning, a water snake is a water snake. So, look down your list of everything called a water snake, and they are all mistaken for all the same!!

The broad-banded water snake is found mostly in the Red River to Gulf eastern one-fourth of Texas.

Water Snake, Diamondback

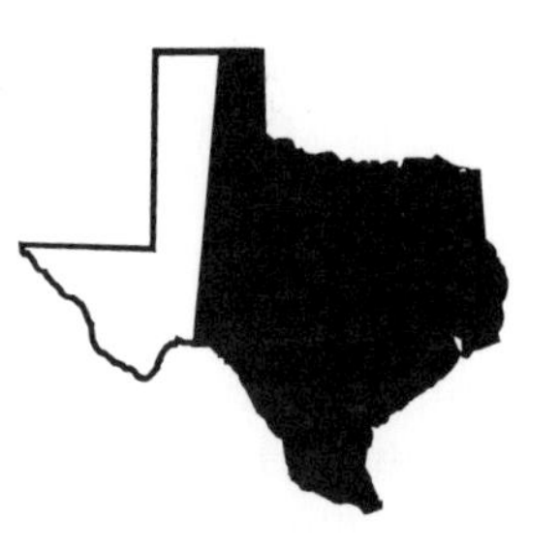

I would just as soon stick my hand into a buzzing Osterizer than to be bitten by this water snake! He is a nasty tempered, foul smelling serpent that will go one better where the bite of a snake is concerned. Most snakes will bite, insert teeth, press, lighten up, and then remove teeth. This snake bites, inserts teeth, then pulls away! You get raked with teeth that are as sharp as needles! Most other snakes will bite and then try to change their location as soon as possible. He will bite, rake, bite, rake, and continue to do so as long as he can reach you! Add to this a foul, no, putrid-smelling musk that can be squirted all over the place. There are nine species of water snake, give or take an opinion, found in Texas and they are all nasty. You'll find them in almost every body of water.

The adult snake appears a solid color from a distance and especially if it is wet. The colors are all ugly and range from black through olive green to tan or brown. The young have a noticeable pattern that can best be described as diamond shaped and chain-like. This pattern is very faint in the adult.

Think yardstick (or meter stick if you are not a Texan) when considering size. These snakes average a little less than 36 inches. They are full bodied but not what you would call stout. All nine species are similar to the water moccasin in appearance. They all look alike in the water. There are very noticeable differences to snake lovers and other crazy people. There is one behavioral difference, but don't bet your appendages on it, which you might lose if the snake doesn't read! When you encounter a harmless water snake he will move out quickly in the direction of the nearest body of water. A poisonous water moccasin will usually coil, raise his head, and stand his ground.

You will find this snake always near the water. It eats frogs, toads, fish, wading birds, ducklings, and anything that comes down to the old water hole for a drink. He will also eat carrion. Here is a joke and I hope you have paid for this book before you read this, because you may not buy the book after you read this! A guy walks up to the ticket counter at the airport. He is carrying a dead armadillo under each arm. The agent asks "Would you like to check those as baggage?" He answers "No, that won't be necessary. These are carrion!"

Water Snake, Yellow-bellied

Like all of its relatives in the water, this animal goes to great lengths to sink his teeth into your anatomy, and he has a smell that can only be topped by an irate skunk. He is nonpoisonous, and in the eastern part of Texas he is the most numerous of the water snakes.

The adult yellow-bellied water snake is a dark grey to almost black. There is a diamond-shaped pattern that is very bright and obvious when this snake is born, but it disappears as it gets older. Not only does this snake have a yellow belly, but the bright yellow seems to creep right from the belly up to ribs on the lower edges.

The adult yellow-bellied water snake averages two and a half feet long. The body is about the diameter of a broomstick.

This snake lives in the water and naturally eats water-dwelling creatures. The adults like fish, frogs, salamanders, and that kind of stuff. The baby snakes dine on tadpoles and aquatic insects.

This snake is a little more diurnal (digs the daylight!) than the other water snakes. He is also one that loves to climb a tree to hang and wait for an unsuspecting fishermen to come on by in a noisy boat, whereupon the snake dives into the boat, causing everybody to jump ship. I'm just kidding here, but I figured you were already thinking about that!!

The fact that one of its preferred food sources, the toad, tends to gather and breed in ditches and little soon-to-be-dried-up ponds will temporarily draw the yellow bellies quite some distance from their home lakes and rivers. This may be one of the reasons that you will uncover one of these snakes deep in the canna plants around your backyard water hydrant!

This may tire you a bit, but he looks like the rest of the water snakes! The others have distinct patterns, but in the water they all look dark and dangerous.

Whip Snake

For you grammar buffs out there the word "whip" in whip snake is an adjective and not a verb! These snakes will be known by their body shape. Think skinny, think long, and think snake. The skinny has a survival reason. This long, thin snake can forage for food during the hottest part of the day because he does not expose large masses of body parts to the elements at any given time. I know what I am trying to say but I think I lost it back there somewhere!

The most common whip snake that allows itself to be seen is dark colored on top and light on the bottom. You will see some white along both sides in the form of small white spots. Two of the species, the desert striped whip snake and the Schott's whip snake, have stripes but are the same long and skinny. The fourth kind, the Ruthven's whip snake, is also a solid color but unless one of those wandered across the border in Brownsville you'd never see one anyway. There is really no discernable pattern in the most common whip snake so think solid color.

The adult size ranges from twenty-eight to seventy-two inches. Even the big ones have a head no bigger than the end of your pointy finger. This is an extremely high strung snake and will "whip" violently when handled. You won't feel like you are on the receiving end of an "Indiana Jones" movie but it will get your attention. They are nonpoisonous but will bite if restrained.

The whip snakes are known to collectors and hobbyists as the lizard eater. You will read in the reference books that they eat rodents but I have never had one show any interest in a mouse. I am sure that is one of your main concerns when being held at bay by a whip snake that has taken up residence in your washroom!

When not looking around your house for a loose, slow lizard this snake prefers thick brushy terrain with lots of debris to hide under. If you really don't like snakes just keep your yard free of brush and debris!

The common Central Texas whip snake is found in West Texas in and on either side a swath of counties from Austin to El Paso.

ALMOST POISONOUS SNAKES

Night Snake

Now don't get your socks in an uproar when I tell you that this snake is mildly venomous. Wait a minute! His saliva — spit for some of us who have this thing about words — has a paralytic effect on the dinky denizens of the dirt that are done in to be devoured. They don't have fangs and usually don't go for the throat. They are found almost everywhere except East Texas but you may never see one. They don't call them night snakes for nothin'.

The colors are not all that exciting to those of you who won't get any closer than the length of your weapon. The main color is light brown or greyish. This is your basic spotted snake and the spots are dark brown, green, or black depending on which crayons you could find to fill in the color chart at the back of the book! The belly is white. There is a dark patch on each side of his neck. He has what looks like eye make-up painted as a dark band backward and down from each eye. Now you really need to look at those eyes. They are big and orange and bulging. The pupils are elliptical like those of a cat.

He is a small snake averaging 10 to 14 inches as an adult. He is the diameter of a good milkshake straw and his head is slightly triangular shaped.

This snake eats mostly lizards but is known to eat earthworms and insects. He likes to burrow and prefers the arid and semiarid habitats of Central and West Texas.

A subspecies, the spotted night snake is very similar and differs, as far as you snake dislikers are concerned, only in shades of color. For those of you who have a vivid imagination and are color blind, you might mistake a Texas brown snake for this one, but it has round eye pupils. I am sure you will notice that right away!

The Texas night snake resides in almost all of the state except for the Big Bend area and East Texas. The spotted night snake is found only in the Big Bend area. If you live in East Texas don't worry too much about night snakes.

Northern Cat-eyed Snake

This snake, like the lyre snake, possesses a pair of slightly enlarged teeth in his upper jaw. The mildly toxic saliva simply flows into the wound made by these teeth. It is strong enough to immobilize small critters that it plans to eat. And, like the lyre snake, that should be enough reason to leave him alone! All you snake experts who believe that any snake can be rendered harmless by picking him up behind the head, listen up! When you try that procedure with this snake beware! Those slightly enlarged teeth are located just about where your thumb and forefinger would be!

This snake is mostly brown or black, with saddle-shaped, cross bands from head to tail. The belly is a light cream or pale yellow. He has a broad head and a menacing look that makes you think of Steven Spielberg movies. It seems to be fixed in a permanent scowl. This snake grows to about two feet long and is relatively thin for its length. He is of the size that he might cause you some pain if he were allowed to swallow your finger far enough to engage the fangs. I'm sure you don't spit into the wind or throw feathers at chickens so I would not think you would allow a snake to swallow your finger!

This animal travels at night in search of a frog or two. He likes the thick vegetation near waterways and ponds.

There may be any number of look-alikes for this snake. The nearest might be the Texas longnose snake. The closer you get, the more different they appear. He is called the Northern cat-eyed snake because his Texas range is the farthest point of his Mexican habitat. He is a resident of the Brownsville area. He is a very secretive snake, so don't expect to be over run by a herd of them.

Texas Lyre Snake

Don't let that name confuse you. Here in Texas you might think I spelled the name wrong. It is not "liar" but it is "lyre" snake. We true Texans could build a whole new volume of folklore around a snake called "liar!" The name has to do with a design on top of his head that looks something like the musical instrument of the same name.

If someone who shares your domicile has one of these for a pet, you may have two points to make. The first thing is that this snake has poison! He uses it to paralyze and immobilize small prey so he can gulp them down. The fangs are really just enlarged, grooved teeth located in his upper jaw. He cannot inject the muscle-pressurized venom that the pit vipers are prone to do. He must swallow the prey animal a short distance before the teeth come into play. The venom is part of his saliva and would not cause much discomfort to a human. You don't have to tell your snake lovin' friend everything!

The next thing you might impart to your weird friend is that this snake has been protected from capture by the Texas Department of Parks and Wildlife since 1977. Should he risk a late night raid? Does he like handcuffs? Does he have $257.50 for a fine, and they want it right now? Does Western Union service Study Butte, Texas? I don't think so.

This snake is a light brown to grey. He has dark brown cross bands that are the shape of little saddles across his back. He has a very distinct neck and a roundish head. It would be "triangular shaped" to those of you who are not snake wise. This snake has elliptical pupils just like your everyday rattlesnake or copperhead.

He prefers to dine upon lizards but will taste-test small mammals and birds. The adults are most often about two feet long. He is not aggressive but will vibrate his tail when picked up.

He can be found at night among the rocks out El Paso way and down into the Big Bend country.

POISONOUS SNAKES

Copperhead

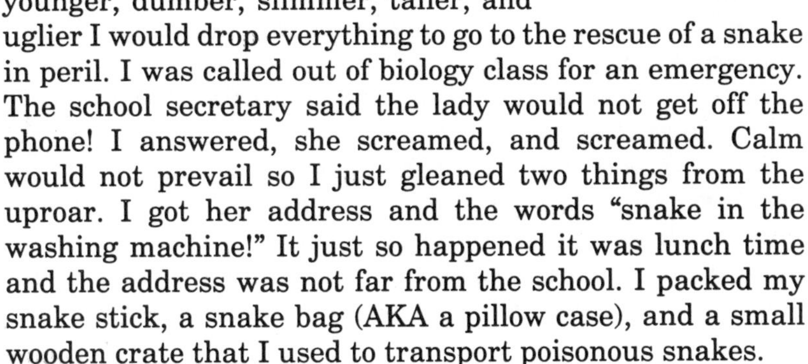

Pay attention now because if this one bites you, it will put a wrinkle in your Dockers! I have a story that I hesitate to tell you because you probably don't get enough sleep as it is. Oh what the hey, I'll tell you anyway!

In the early days when I was younger, dumber, slimmer, taller, and uglier I would drop everything to go to the rescue of a snake in peril. I was called out of biology class for an emergency. The school secretary said the lady would not get off the phone! I answered, she screamed, and screamed. Calm would not prevail so I just gleaned two things from the uproar. I got her address and the words "snake in the washing machine!" It just so happened it was lunch time and the address was not far from the school. I packed my snake stick, a snake bag (AKA a pillow case), and a small wooden crate that I used to transport poisonous snakes.

I arrived and she was standing at the front door with her mouth open and pointing inside. She looked me over because I must have reminded her of a character from "Ghost Busters." I sort of knew what to expect, but I always enjoy the drama of the situation so I played it to the hilt. "Is there anyone else in the house?" "No," she answered. "I'll have to close this door because I don't want any distractions while I work." She asked, "Where do you want me to be?" I frowned and looked dead serious, "I'll call you when I finish." "No problem," she said as she beat a hasty retreat. I closed the door behind me, put all that junk down, and opened the lid on the Kenmore. "I seen the snake!" "I seen the snake." That still sounds right! There he was. It was a small copperhead just laying there minding his own business. If he could think, he would be thinking that it is a bad idea to crawl into just any old pipe you see sticking out. He was only about eight inches long and obviously a newborn. And, wouldn't you know it, my snake stick was too big to pick him up! Great, I'll get the frantic lady back into the act. I yelled. I heard a faint reply. I opened the door and asked her for a wire coat hanger. She brought one and handed it to me as if I were the snake! To make a long story even longer, I fashioned a hook from the coat hanger and removed the snake and put it into the wooden lock box.

It took me a while to convince the homeowner that this was a once-in-a-lifetime occurrence. The little snake had crawled up the drain pipe from under the house and into the washer tub. Mother copperhead was long gone and all the brothers and sisters were most likely headed for parts unknown. She wanted that in writing but I don't write (you suspected that already!).

About the last part of the fall season and just before you are forced to pick up all those leaves, just look at them. Imagine those colors on a snake. That is the color of a copperhead. You might also think of the snake laying on top or under those leaves and how well he blends in. Use gloves and a rake!

The pattern can be described as rough edged, uneven bands that stretch across the snake. Think "hourglass" shaped designs. His belly is pale yellow with mottled reddish brown.

A copperhead the length of a yardstick would be one heck of a big copperhead! Most of them are in the two-foot range. If you see one, you should look at his two feet and use your two feet to vacate the area!

The copperhead likes the leaf litter on the forest floor for hiding, hunting, and making more copperheads. He prefers to eat mice but will dine on frogs, lizards, an occasional toad, and sometimes another snake. He is a laid-back creature that wants to be left alone. When he senses your presence he will flatten his body and freeze. This is to maximize his dead leaf camouflage. If he sees he's been seen, he will raise his head, strike, and vibrate his tail. Take a hint and a hike!

There are three species of copperhead that you might find in Texas, and all of them are basically alike in appearance but the colors may be lighter or darker. The hognose snake when viewed from above is a similar snake. The hognose has a wide neck when compared to the thin, well-defined neck of the copperhead.

The three species (did I already say that?): the southern copperhead, the broad-banded copperhead, and Trans-Pecos copperhead combined geographical range covers all of the state except the El Paso area. If you are really afraid of copperheads, I know a real estate agent in El Paso!

Coral Snake

Over the years I have had on hand a lot of different kinds of poisonous snakes. I have been paranoid all these years that one of them would escape and my career would end. There will be some truth here so watch for cloudy skies and don't stand on a hill or under a tree! I have had one poisonous snake escape. Yes it was a coral snake. Here is my story. The names have not been changed to protect the innocent. I don't know any innocent people so that doesn't really bother me!

It was a dark and stormy night. It might have been, I don't remember. The room at the high school was dark and even the custodian had gone home. The captive coral snake came out from under his piece of tree bark on the floor of his aquarium habitat. He then began pursuing his ancestral instinctive commands to roam. He tried every barrier at least once. On the second time around, or it may have happened on the first time around but I'm writing this bit! Anyway, the snake found a hole. It seemed that whoever was in charge of the aquarium cages had put a top on this one that had a pencil-sized hole. The dummy!

The snake placed his head through the hole and that is all it took. If you are a coral snake, your body is the same diameter as your head. He was free at last. That did not matter much to the snake, because he did not realize he was a captive in the first place! He moved and he moved and he moved. Suddenly the lights came on. He sensed the approaching two-hundred pound, six-foot, three-inch biology teacher, and he moved quickly under the cabinet on his left. Sounds like I was there doesn't it?

This is where I jump in. I noticed the last two inches of his red, yellow, and black ringed body disappear under the sink cabinet. The cabinet had a false bottom and was anchored to the floor. I had to work quickly because I knew the snake would not stop there. I raced to the custodian room and borrowed one of those two-wheeled loading dollies. I put the edge of the dolly under the corner of the cabinet and used it as a crowbar. I pulled down on the handle and things began to pop, break, and groan. No snake. I whipped out my flashlight and noticed that there was a one-quarter-inch crack around the base of the water pipe that went through the floor. Oh boy! This school had a basement that stretched the length of the building. I raced to the basement. I found the pipe that led to my room and no snake!

Do I tell the principal? What would he do? He would have to close the school and send 2200 students home with a story of how a dumb biology teacher let a poisonous snake loose! No good.

The floor was about one foot thick so here was my brilliant idea. I would mix up a big bag of Quik-crete and fill in the space. The coral snake would be entombed forever! In thirty or forty years he might become as famous as "Old Rip," the horned toad. I did all that. As I stood there admiring my somewhat sloppy work it occurred to me that the snake may have already slipped into the basement before I plugged the hole. I was dead!

I marched right into Mr. Sherman Millander's office and sat down. He looked at me and thanked me for knocking. He began the conversation as usual. "Dunlap, whatever it is, I don't want to know!" Mr. Millander had been my principal for almost all of my teaching career. He and I had an understanding. If I sold candy in the halls and used the profits for animal care, don't tell him. If I talked the Vocational Agriculture Department into building a weird animal cage for me, don't tell him. If I traded, sold, bought, or borrowed in the name of the school, don't tell him! He was usually ready for something when he saw me. I whimpered, "Well sir, that philosophy has worked for us for the last ten years and I have succeeded in getting into and out of trouble all by myself, but this time...." He sensed there was real trouble because he stopped smiling. I blurted out the story. He looked at his watch and it was only early afternoon. He said, "Let's go look." We started toward the basement with Mr. Albert French, the school head custodian. Mr. French knew more about the building than the building contractor. We walked down into the bowels of the basement. In the semidarkness we stepped around old desks, over tables and stored drill team props. We all looked up in unison toward the pipe that led to my room. The wet concrete had seeped through the cracks around the pipe. We all made some kind of sound when we noticed a flash of color in the grey slop of Quik-crete. The coral snake was on his way out! Mr. French handed me a drill-team stool that was not meant to hold a two-hundred-pound person with all his clothes on! I assumed that one of these grown men would steady the stool. They had disappeared! From a spot about fifty yards away and near the door I heard a faint, "Be careful!" I found a piece of wire on the ground and quickly fashioned a snake hook in one end. I stepped up on the stool and reached carefully up and hooked the snake through the exposed coil. One quick jerk, one grunt (from me), and two loud gasps (from them) and the snake was on the ground! I flipped him into a big tin can and declared the world "safe!"

The colors of this snake are the easy part of the identification. They are perfectly ringed with red, yellow, and black. There are no "ishes" to these colors. The rings go completely around the snake. These rings are different widths. The red being the widest, the black next, and the yellow being the narrowest.

A big coral snake may measure 36 inches. He will be about the diameter of your ring finger. His head is small and there is not an obvious neck. He is a shy, docile creature that hardly ever comes out of his crack in the ground or rotting log. He eats mostly small snakes and skinks. Skinks are small lizards that look like snakes.

The Texas coral snake has very short fangs and must chew its prey to inject the venom. One layer of cloth is usually enough protection from the bite of a coral snake. You should know better than to run naked in the woods.

There are two similar snakes you might run across in Texas. One is the red milk snake and the other is the scarlet snake. They have red, yellow, and black bands like the coral snake. The coral snake has red and yellow bands that come together and the harmless milk snakes and scarlet snakes have red and black bands that touch. Remember that!

The coral snake can be found everywhere east and south of a line from Texarkana to Langtry.

Water Moccasin

The water moccasin suffers from bad press. A small percentage of the yearly snake bites in Texas involve the cottonmouth. The statistics show that the mortality rate throughout the United States is "less than one person per year." Should we stop here and look into that statement? What would this person look like? Maybe later!

Oh where to start! Think of the scene in the movie "Lonesome Dove" where the cowboy falls into the river. The water starts to jump like you see in a piranha attack. The cowboy is pulled to the shore and rolled over to expose multiple fang marks all over the place. He dies on the spot. We Texans love that stuff! The cowboy obviously fell into a "nest" of water moccasins. Stop!

There are only two times when you might see more than one water moccasin in one place at one time. During the mating season you will see two. If I need to explain that one, you are reading the wrong book! The other time is when the mama moccasin is giving birth to her young. It is a live birth and she may have 3 to 12 at one sitting. The babies might hang around to watch or something and hence you have a "nest" of snakes. They have never been known to "gang attack" anything!

I don't fish. It takes patience to sit there and wait. I'll sit for about ten minutes and then I put down the pole and wander down the bank turning over stuff to look for snakes. I do appreciate fish stories, especially the ones where snakes are involved. Here it is: "Waell, me and Billy Bob wus putterin' down the creek, trollin' a lit'l, lookin' for tha spot. Somethin' jumped outta tha tree and purt near hit ol' Billy Bob inna face! He hollered an' stood up real quick like. He kept right on goin' and went head first in tha creek! I heered 'im holler "snake!" and then I seen it. It uz a big ol' cottonmouth musta been six foot long! It skert me sa bad I jumped up nigh belly high and come down in tha water too! Me and Billy Bob swum to shore and jus sat there lookin' at dat boat wonderin' how it wus we's gonna git our stuff back!"

That snake "attack" might have occurred but not with the same intent. Water moccasins as well as other water snakes like to sun themselves on low hanging branches. If they sense danger, they instinctively go for the water. If there happens to be a boat between them and safety, so be it.

As a baby, the cottonmouth water moccasin is brightly colored with greens, browns, and yellows. As they get older the color and diamond pattern fades to various shades of black, green, and brown. The pattern is most visible along the side of the adult snake.

I won't try to write accent again but the "size" story is really good. "The cottonmouth was stretched completely across the road and was as big around as a man's thigh." Our western cottonmouth averages 20 inches. The record in Texas now stands at 60 inches. The cottonmouth is short and stout for its length. The head is noticeably triangular shaped and the eyes face forward.

The cottonmouth gets its name because of a peculiar behavior when threatened. He will coil, raise his head, and yawn. I have been known to do that at family gatherings. The inside of his mouth is as white as cotton. That could be a signal of alarm, a warning meant to be intimidating, or he really is bored. Who knows!

If the snake is pinned down, he will spray a foul-smelling musk from anal glands at the base of his tail. The mist created is overwhelming. That reminds me of another story. Aren't you happy? During the morning "get ready" ritual at my house I happened to pass by the bathroom door. My daughter was moving around inside and caught my attention. She had a spray bottle in one hand, and as I watched she misted the air in front of her. She then quickly walked through the mist! She answered my obvious question by saying that she was following instructions. This particular fragrance had to be applied in that manner. Maybe that company was established by a former snake hunter!

The cottonmouth loves frogs but will take small mammals, birds, and even other snakes. If you hear a fish story about a cottonmouth coming up on the pier and eating fish guts, well, that one is true. You can also assume that a water moccasin can bite under water. He eats water dwelling creatures, so if he could not bite under water, he would starve.

Your mind and up-bringing will tell you that every snake that you see in the water is a water moccasin. There are no less than nine species of harmless water snakes in our Texas waters, and all of them could be mistaken for a moccasin. If you should see a cottonmouth water moccasin on or near your dock or pier, there is only one thing to do. Move!

The Texas cottonmouth water moccasin is found in the eastern half of the state. It does not live in the southern parts of the state. It kinda figures don't it?

PESKY PETS

So a significant one who shares your domicile has decided it would be nice to have a boa constrictor or a python as a pet. You have fought and argued against it but to no avail. There are some arguments you can try to dissuade this person from bringing a snake into the house.

You might try the old it's-illegal tactic. Most cities have ordinances that prohibit keeping anything called a boa constrictor or a python. The rationale being these animals get quite large and can be dangerous. Ha! If that is the case I have two illegal teenagers! And if that argument doesn't work, it is possible to coexist with a snake in the house.

Let's talk about the advantages. When it's time for the company to leave, just start saying things like "Did you remember to lock Fang's cage?" And then there might be "don't forget to thaw a rat for Miss Hiss" Another advantage is that you can file for divorce at any time. Also you will find very soon that in-laws become nonexistent.

There are, of course, some disadvantages. For example, loaded guns lying around the house can be hazardous to your health. The officer asks "Why did you pull the trigger?" You answer, "I thought it was the snake!" Another might be having to lead a life in the paranoid zone. You have to deal with terms like escape, crush, bite, and the subsequent disappearance of family pets. You might also find that you've lost use of one or more bedrooms. There may be a time when you have to ask the question, "He has escaped? Now what?"

We will begin by discussing some of these snakes and as you might expect I always have a story. The first snake I want to talk about is the boa constrictor. Whenever you see something on television concerning a snake, that snake is almost always identified as a boa constrictor. It seems that the word constrictor strikes fear in the hearts of all those people who are afraid of snakes. First of all they figure if it's not venomous, then it must crush you to death.

Let's begin with my story. In my early years as a biology teacher I always had a lot of snakes in my classroom. It was always a challenge to me to identify an ophidiophobic student and then to "cure" them. I remember Joyce who was a very energetic, bright, devil-may-care young lady who loved school. She didn't like snakes. Her degree plan had been changed around too many times, and now it came down to biology at a certain time, semester, and course number. It had to be my class. She came to me during registration and pleaded her case. She begged that I try and make some arrangement for her to do her work somewhere else besides my classroom with all those snakes. After much coercion, promises of extra work, and maybe her firstborn child, we worked out a procedure. She would enter my class through an adjacent classroom, sit at the midpoint of the double room, right in the path of the sliding accordion wall. I would make an effort to come to her and she would stay put. We would work out lab problems as they arose. Joyce started all her sentences with the word "like." She punctuated the end of her sentences with "ya know." I have no intention of classifying her but, like, she was a cheerleader, ya know? I try not to single out a student after learning something about them but Joyce asked for it.

The first day she arrived right on time, and when the bell rang all her friends scattered like startled quail. She just sat there staring straight ahead. All the cages of snakes were located toward the sides of the classroom and near the front. I removed those cages from her immediate area. The semester moved on and after a while the stark fear in her eyes gave way to an uneasy calm. She began to look around a little more. I welcomed that because as a high school teacher I was not used to having any student stare at me as if they were paying attention. Most of my chapter-to-chapter lessons eventually moved to reptiles as examples and to snakes in particular. I assigned teams of students to an animal that they would use for a two-week project.

They were to do research which included all aspects of the animal's existence. The care of the animal was also their responsibility. Of course Joyce had no intention of being assigned to work on a snake as a project. I did at the time have some hamsters and gerbils, and I decided she could use those as her particular project. No, they were not snake hors d'oeuvres!

The semester wore on and eventually she began working in the classroom not really paying much attention to the snakes. When I would take a snake around to the students, she would actually stand her ground and not try to leave the room. Eventually she actually began to ask questions about the snakes. She even watched one of them eat a mouse and I felt we were making progress. One particular day when I had a rather large python on the table Joyce decided to come forward. All the students in the class knew of her fear, and it suddenly became very silent and everybody stood and looked at Joyce. Without any coaxing whatsoever she walked slowly and quietly toward the table; to my amazement she extended her hand and touched the snake. From that point on it was total fascination on Joyce's part. She would touch a snake at every opportunity.

It was only the next day that she decided, I've touched it, I can hold it. She walked up, I laid the snake in her hands, she stood there for a moment, her eyes got very large, and then I noticed what looked like love at first sight. From that point on Joyce was totally infatuated with that snake. She would come to class and ask very politely if she could hold the snake. She wanted to hold the snake while she was doing her work. I thought there would be no harm in that, and so every day when she came to class she would sit there with that small boa constrictor in her lap or pocket or somewhere on the desk.

One day things were going as usual; Joyce came in, took the snake out of the aquarium, sat down, and began working on a work sheet. All of a sudden I noticed some of her friends had gathered around her and were whispering excitedly. Joyce got up and with her entourage walked quietly to the front of the room. She seemed to be holding her stomach as if she were sick. She had a strange look in her eyes. She whispered to me, "Mr. Dunlap, can I go to the restroom?" I said I would let her go down there but the rest was up to her! That's a real old teacher response. It is supposed to be funny.

I asked if there was a problem, and she leaned a little closer and whispered that the little boa constrictor had crawled into her blouse and gotten tangled in her bra. I don't normally laugh "at" students in class, but I believe I guffawed a bit and she was embarrassed. She returned after a while and all seemed to be well. That particular situation seemed to be the running classroom joke for the rest of the semester.

Pythons

Second to the boa constrictors in the area of bad press, lies, myths, and stories are a group of snakes called the pythons. The pythons include both the giants and the dwarfs, but most people have been programmed to believe that all pythons get 40 feet long and weigh 500 pounds. The largest reticulated python may grow to thirty feet and weigh 300 pounds but you will have gotten rid of him long before he gets that big. Most all of the pythons are confined to the tropics of Africa, Asia, and Australia. We don't have pythons native to the United States and we certainly don't have any pythons native to Texas.

Pythons are interesting in a number of ways but, of course, if you are being forced to live with one, it may not make any difference to you.

One of the things that come up at parties quite frequently is that boas and pythons are very primitive snakes. The example of this is that they actually have toenails, and they also have a primitive pelvic girdle to which legs were once attached. The toenails are in the form of a pair of cloacal spurs, which simply means these toenails are located on either side of the anal opening at the tail end of the snake. These toenails have evolved to being used during courtship and copulation. The present day function of these spurs is not really that unusual among people; it is a little strange among snakes. Whenever a male and female are considering making babies the male will actually entwine the female, and with those spurs extended he will scratch her on the back. This in some way stimulates her into copulation. Pythons are egg layers as opposed to the boa constrictors that give birth to live, ready-to-go, babies.

Pythons are also one of the few reptiles that actually participate in the incubation of the eggs. The pythons, after they have laid their egg clutch, which stick together forming a large ball of eggs, will actually coil around their eggs for varying lengths of time. Several of the larger species, especially one we'll talk about, the Burmese, are known to remain with their eggs for the full incubation period of around two months. They incubate them by raising their own body temperature. This is accomplished through muscular contractions. They jerk and quiver and by doing so can raise the temperature inside the coil.

The pet shop guy might sell you something about three feet long and call it a Burmese rock snake. It is illegal in most cities to own a python, therefore the name is changed. When you ask how big it will grow, you will be told, "Oh, not very big!" If you are the one considering the purchase of a pet snake, you should read about them first. This book will help.

African Ball Python

This is probably the most sought after and purchased pet python on the market today. The main reason it is so popular is that it usually does not get over 3 feet long, and it is a shy, quiet, retiring animal that doesn't bite. They are easily maintained and they really do make good pets if you are a snake person.

The name ball python comes from the fact that when you disturb, pick up, or frighten the snake it coils up into a tight ball and will put its head right down in the center of the coils. He then is coiled so tightly that you will be tempted to toss him around just like a ball. In Africa, where the ball python is found, they prefer to live in mammal burrows and holes that are found around tree trunks and also in rock crevices. The ball python is an egg-laying snake. The female will coil around the eggs as do a lot of the pythons. She may remain with them for two to three months of incubation, which is usually required for hatching.

Ball pythons, unfortunately, are very popular in their native country for two reasons. First of all, the tribal people really love them as a food source, and they are collected for their skins which are sold for making billfolds, purses, etc. The sad situation that occurs in pet shops is that these animals are imported directly from being caught in the wild. An adult ball python is very, very difficult to maintain in captivity. As a matter of fact, most people who purchase them will wait up to two years before they decide to get some professional help with their fasting snake. By that time it is usually too late.

The ball python currently housed in my school collection is one that I have had longer than any other snake in the collection. His name is Chicken and I've had him for 17 years. I got him a few days after he hatched from an egg. He was given to me by a friend at the Dallas Zoo. I named him Chicken because he seemed to be afraid of everything and he is very shy. He always hides his eyes with a coiled body as if to say, "Don't hurt me."

Anyway, when Chicken was quite small he was about as big around as a thumb and about a foot long. He was being used, as were all my animals in the collection, as a classroom project. I remember the young man who was charged with feeding and caring for Chicken during that period. He happened to be a very, very large football player. It was the football player's senior year and, of course, as all seniors do, he had a very pretty class ring. I remember this young man's class ring for two reasons. First of all, this kid weighed 250 pounds and was 6'6" tall. Consequently, this ring he had on his hand took on the weight and measurement of something very large. The football player was sitting in class one day, holding Chicken while working on his report, when he sauntered up to the desk and placed Chicken on the desk in front of me and whispered in my ear, "Mr. Dunlap, we have a problem here." I looked at him, I looked at the snake and said, "What's wrong? He said, "I was playing with Chicken and I decided that he might want to crawl through my class ring." Chicken had crawled partway through his class ring, and the ring became lodged about midbody and wouldn't move up or down. For the next hour or so we had a lot of fun with hand soap, then vaseline, and finally, one of the students in the classroom had some very expensive, very slick hand lotion. We simply slicked Chicken up with hand lotion and the ring finally came off. From that point on, without getting too tacky with the huge football player, I suggested that he not do anything like that again.

The color of a ball python is basically black. On the black are very distinctive circles and patterns of mostly yellow. The pattern of the ball python is intriguing simply because when you look at the round patches of yellowish scales they take on the appearance of a mask one might wear to a halloween ball. Using a little more imagination, you might also say that they look something like the face of E.T. They are quite distinctive and are on all ball pythons. The colors of the ball python do not vary other than some are darker than others. They tend to be very brightly colored upon hatching, and as they get older the colors fade and they become quite a bit darker. As I have mentioned before, the ball python hardly ever gets over three feet long. A five-footer would certainly be an exception.

Burmese Python

Now we'll discuss that giant python that is currently making one room of your house uninhabitable. The Burmese python appears regularly in pet shops, usually for an outrageous sum of money. It is always a small 3- or 4-foot, beautiful snake sitting there neatly in its ten-gallon aquarium. The pet shop person goes to great lengths to convince you it is docile, easy to get along with, and "doesn't bite," and does well in any home situation. The Burmese python is native to Southeast Asia and countries like Thailand, Vietnam, Burma — those sorts of places.

In their natural habitat in today's world they are suffering quite a bit from the fact that natives consider them a delicacy. A large python will make a meal for a small family and consequently they are hunted. In some areas where a little more understanding is prevalent the animals are protected because it is known that they help keep down the rodent population which, of course, runs all over the thatched hut community. So, in some areas they are quite beneficial.

The Burmese python is a heavy bodied and colorful animal. A pattern of large, reddish-brown blotches are outlined in cream or gold, and the ground color is usually a pale green or tan. The hatchlings are usually the ones you buy in the pet shop and are about 18 inches long and as big around as a quarter. Those hatchlings will grow somewhere in the neighborhood of one foot per year and may attain a length of 25 feet. Ordinarily, though, 18 to 20 feet would be the norm. Try to imagine an 18-foot python living in the house. When you say he just lays around what you really mean is that he literally "lays around the house!"

Burmese pythons prey upon mammals, birds, and reptiles of appropriate sizes. The stories you may hear that they eat water buffalo and small giraffes and antelope are just so much poo. Although that has been known to occur, that is not their particular preference for food items. There has never been, as of this writing, a substantiated record of a python swallowing a human being. One of the neatest photos that I have seen in recent years was on the cover of one of the grocery store tabloids. This large black and white picture showed a very large python with an unsightly lump in the middle of its body. There were natives standing on either side of the animal and one of the natives seemed to be pointing at the large lump and the caption read "Raoul." From those kinds of photos and that kind of narrative one can see where the swallowing-people myth is proliferated.

During my biology teaching days I maintained a large population of caged snakes in the classroom. I do remember one instance where a Burmese python became very important. The incident is still brought to mind every time I visit with Katy. Katy is my favorite Burmese python. She is now almost 18 feet long and weighs over 200 pounds. When Katy was only about 4 feet long, which was probably a couple of years after I got her as a hatchling, I maintained her in a rather large wooden box with a glass front. The box sat on a table near the front of my classroom near my desk. One of the ways I fed all of my reptiles was by depending upon donations. One of my sources of donated rats, mice, and rabbits was one of the local hospitals. The hospital was a teaching, research hospital and consequently they used rodents for various activities. Doctors would practice reconnecting arteries and veins as part of their surgical training. I had always gotten rats from this institution, and most all the rats were euthanized by gassing using carbon dioxide.

On one occasion I got my usual packaged rats from the hospital, and in one lone plastic bag there were two rather large rats. Not really thinking anything about it, I thawed one of those rats and one afternoon before I left for home I fed one to Katy. Katy, of course, being the instinctual animal that she is, grabbed, constricted, released, and swallowed the large white rat. Upon arriving in the classroom the next morning, I noticed Katy lying full length on the bottom of the cage.

Ordinarily, as I walk by the front of the cage she would react; she would turn or flick her tongue. I noticed she didn't move so I opened the door of the cage, and to my horror Katy was dead. My thoughts immediately went to the rat that I had given her the night before, and immediately I thought about how that rat may have been euthanized. Two plus two equals four and I said to myself, "I've killed one of my snakes." It was time for the bell to ring and I knew that I would not have time to dispose of Katy right away. As the students came into class I just ignored the situation. Although she was dead she looked alive because of the way she was lying. Later in the class period I just couldn't keep the news to myself so I informed the class of the situation. They, of course, were quite sad because Katy had become the classroom pet.

Class droned on and I was lecturing when all of a sudden one of my students sitting at the front table screamed. I remember the young lady very well. Her name was Kelly Russell, and she was one of the biggest fans of Katy because she played with her almost on a daily basis. She screamed and that got everybody's attention. She said, "Katy breathed." I went over and opened the cage, and yes, Katy was breathing. She only took a breath every few seconds but there was life in the snake. What I assumed had happened was that the rat must have been euthanized with some sort of tranquilizing drug. When it entered Katy's system she didn't die but her metabolism slowed to comatose. She was slowly waking up, and by the end of the day Katy was her old self again. From that time on I made it a point to question the technicians who gave me the rats. I had to be sure that if the rats were euthanized by some other method than carbon dioxide gas, I would not use those rats as snake food.

Reticulated Python

Almost everyone who dabbles in snake-maintaining activity has had some sort of run-in with a reticulated python. On almost every occasion whenever someone is trying to donate or give me their snake, they always seem to emphasize that it is very tame and doesn't bite. One of the outstanding characteristics of reticulated pythons is that they are very, very aggressive.

Their food drive is just enormous. They can grow three feet a year and it is not unusual for a five-year-old to be 9 or 10 feet long. They are aggressive and eventually anyone who buys one will have large teeth marks in their hand or arm. If they are snake lovers, they won't mention it; if they're borderline snake people, you'll hear about it right away. The references go so far as to recommend that if you own one of these large snakes, that you do not handle the animal unless there are at least two people. Upon hearing that I would think that most intelligent people would simply move on to something else.

The reticulated python gets it name from the fact that the pattern is very complicated and the reticulated has to do with the way the diamond shaped patches are arranged along its back. The snake is a basic light green. The complicated pattern consists of large diamond shaped patches of brown, orange, and black.

The reticulated python is one that reaches the longest length of almost all snakes. The anaconda of South America is the only other snake that attains a larger size. These animals can grow to over 30 feet long and weigh 400 to 500 pounds. Most people who buy them as pets have no idea of the size that can be reached by this snake. Consequently, whenever they reach between 10 and 15 feet it's time to find some other place for them to live.

In captivity the food requirements for the reticulated python can be sometimes overwhelming, because the large snakes will feed on full-grown rabbits, chickens, etc. Reticulated pythons are so aggressive in their feeding behavior that they sometimes will eat prepared processed meat in the form of frozen chicken that you buy at the grocery store. Upon receiving one of these animals as a donation I would immediately start calling all of my friends who are snake collectors trying to get rid of it.

I had a retic brought in one morning before class and I decided to use that animal as part of a demonstration. I lifted the 6-foot snake from the cage. He was coiled, and knowing his aggressive behavior I thought it would be neat if I could just pick him up in his coiled position. I would then hold him in front of me in front of the class and do the presentation. I lifted the animal up about eye level, and as I was speaking I looked off to the side. When I looked back at the snake his very wide open mouth was coming at a very fast speed directly at my eyes. I moved quicker that moment than I have ever moved in my life. I pushed the snake away and down to the desk top and stepped back. Because of my reaction, the snake snapped and simply got a lot of air and I was very happy about that. I suddenly remembered, while in my training and learning about snakes, being told that even in the wild this animal, when it strikes, goes almost always for the area of the eyes.

Think at least three times before you take on a reticulated python as a pet. Even then don't do it!

South American Boa Constrictor

The boa constrictor has suffered from bad press over the years primarily due to the TV jungle movies. These always had wildly adventurous stories that usually had a scene where the ferocious boa constrictor leaped from the trees in the jungle onto the unsuspecting Jungle Jim as he walked down the trail. After listening to sounds of crunch and crackle the hero lay mortally wounded while the horrible arch villain slid out through the jungle and into the trees.

Actually, the boa constrictor is probably the most docile of the "giant snakes." They do not drop out of trees. For that matter, they don't even live in trees. They certainly do not devour people, including heroes and heroines, nor do they like water buffalo or other large animals. They do not get as large as the press seems to like to indicate. The boa would not even try an oversize meal simply because the ingestion of such a large-sized meal would make the boa virtually helpless and unable to defend itself. It would be "might near" impossible to escape from predators, simply because it could not drag around such a large meal.

They do kill their prey by constriction, but they do not crush the food animal. It is a matter of simply applying intense pressure of the constricting coil, and it prevents both the heart and lungs from functioning. It causes almost instantaneous unconsciousness and subsequently the death of the prey.

The colors exhibited by the common boa constrictor of South America can best be described as mostly yellowish-orange. Then there are large patches of darker tannish-red skin along their backs. They are quite colorful. I particularly admire the fact that they have a racing stripe down each side of their head going from the eye back to the chin bone. There are dark and light phases of this snake but the patterns are basically the same, sometimes harder to see with the darker colored animal.

The known maximum length of boas varies greatly because there are so many different kinds, each has its own particular average length. The South American forms of this animal hardly ever reach eight feet and the record is a little over 18 feet. That, folks, is a very uncommon and very rare length. You can expect the adult common boa constrictor to approach a length of 10 feet. They reach a diameter of 6 to 10 inches depending upon how much they eat and how they are raised.

Boas prey on a wide variety of mammals and birds. The young boas are born alive and average 15 to 20 inches long. These are the ones that you can buy in the pet shops and usually the pet shop owner will tell you that they only get 5 or 6 feet long.

One of the common misconceptions about snakes is that they require live food. That situation can be dangerous for a captive animal for the very simple reason that even in the wild, when a snake grabs a potential dinner, it sometimes will be bitten by the prey. In the wild, the movement of the snake keeps the wound clean and avoids infection. In a captive situation where the snake is forced to live with the moisture from the water bowl, feces that do not get cleaned, and not being allowed to move around freely, can set up an infection site very easily. So, it is always best to feed the snake dead prey, and that would be in the form of rats and mice that can be easily kept in the freezer. It is a simple matter to thaw one out when feeding time rolls around. Oh yes, my children, it's story time!

I taught high school biology for eight years, and during that time I maintained a collection of snakes. I used these animals for classroom projects. Seems like I have told you this before. Well anyway, I kept frozen mouse-and-rat-sicles in a classroom freezer. When time to feed came I would place a little "snakey TV dinner" in a plain brown paper bag and stroll over to the Home Economics class next door. A few seconds in the microwave did the trick! One day I took out a large rat which was of questionable origin and placed it in the bag and then on to home-eco. I put the microwave on the usual couple of minutes. It seems the rat had been frozen at a time when it was already a bit ripe! His stomach exploded and the inside of the microwave was....well, I'll leave it there! To this day that teacher will not speak to me!

If you or the person who lives with you decides to get a boa constrictor as a pet, you might question this person about what will happen to the boa when interest wanes or the situation around the house changes. I get calls frequently saying the owner of the snake has moved away to college or has gotten a divorce or is no longer taking care of the snake, etc. The caller is usually frantic because it's always the caller who is deathly afraid of the snake. You might establish some ground rules before you take on a boa constrictor as a pet.

SLITHERIN' LIZARDS

So you thought you had rendered a snake to mincemeat, but on closer examination something didn't seem right. There are three lizards that live in Texas that do not have legs! There are some noticeable differences between these "legless" lizards and snakes. If the animal in question is still alive and you have the time to look him in the eye, you will notice he will wink. Lizards have eyelids and snakes do not. Lizards also have ears in the form of little holes on either side of their heads; snakes do not. To the touch these lizards feel stiff and brittle. They lack the suppleness of the snake. And you thought you would never use the term "suppleness" and "snake" in the same sentence, ha! These lizards also have tails that measure over twice the length of their head and body. For those of you that think that a snake is tail from right behind their jaws to the tip, well, au contraire! The tail of a snake starts at the anal opening which is located, you guessed it, near the tail of the snake.

The legless lizards are extremely fragile. It is uncommon to collect a full-tailed animal. Most of them have a regenerated tail tip that is noticeable because it is a different color from the rest of the critter. If the tail is struck sharply with a blunt object, it will break into one or more pieces. Folklore has given this animal the name of "joint snake" or "glass lizard" because of this adaptation. It was also believed that the lizard could, after a period of time, join the broken parts back together. Most all our Texas lizards are capable of regenerating a lost tail. This loss is a defense mechanism which leaves a predator with a tail in his mouth while the main body of the lizard has taken off to safer places.

Slender Glass Lizard

The only outstanding incident I can remember concerning a glass lizard falls in the category of "What are the odds of that happening?" Throughout my animal related life I have bartered, traded, finagled, accepted, and otherwise received various critters. I have pursued these activities in places like dark alleys, service stations on lonely highways, and an occasional Dairy Queen. I really enjoyed meeting total strangers in these places to trade snakes, pick up a coyote pup, or take in a hurt owl.

Before I became famous and fabulously wealthy writing this book (ha! ha! ha!), I would moonlight at various jobs in an effort to make ends meet. One of the jobs that could have been exciting but wasn't was the time I was employed as a "Rent-a-cop." I was a security officer. I wore the blue and carried the gun. As I think back on that time it really scares me that I carried a gun!

I was assigned an evening gig at a luxury hotel in downtown Dallas, Texas. There was a convention of television executives, and there were supposed to be some celebrities on hand. The only thing that mattered to me was that a person was driving through Dallas from South Texas en route to yankee country to live and work. He had a slender glass lizard that he raised from a hatchling and wanted to find it a good home. I was more than happy to accommodate him.

We met at a prearranged time in the lobby. We spotted each other and moved clandestinely to the nearest potted plant. As a security officer I would have busted us for a drug buy if I had observed the same activity. We looked sneaky, we acted sneaky, and we passed something snaky between us. It was mid-February and the outside temperature was in the teens. This person had the lizard inside his shirt unconfined! The lizard, a beautiful one I might add, was coiled in a semihibernation state and just was not moving. I transferred him to the inside of my shirt, bade goodbye and good luck in yankee land to the operative, and we parted.

My shift was to be over in about an hour so I figured the lizard would be safe in my shirt. He was too cold to move. I took the elevator and was headed back to the main ballroom on the fourth floor. The lizard was causing no more notice than an unsightly bulge in my shirt which could have been mistaken for just "rolls of me!"

There were two other people in the elevator car and my first inclination was to do my favorite experiment in human behavior. I have been known to enter the elevator, push my floor button, and then turn and face the other passengers. You all know that standard operating procedure is to turn and look at the little lighted numbers above the door.

I didn't do that. I turned and faced the numbers just like I was expected to do. The elevator stopped at the second floor. The doors opened. My mouth opened! This old guy about four feet tall and chewing on a cigar stepped into the car and turned to face the little lighted numbers. It was George Burns! Blub! Blub! I forgot all about the lizard. "Good evening Mr. Burns, could I have your autograph?" I blurted. "I'd be glad to but I don't have a pen" he said. The three of us nobody's began slapping pockets in hopes that a nonexistent writing instrument would magically appear. There was none! "I have always enjoyed your work" I said. "Thank you" he said. Ding! the door opened and he walked out.

Now I ask you. What are the odds? Me, dressed in a cop uniform, a cold slender glass lizard under my shirt, sharing an elevator car with George Burns, and not one pen among four people! Life is grand.

The slender glass lizard is yellowish brown. There are thin, dark, parallel stripes down his back that show a light yellow color in the background. The belly is yellow. There are a few flecks of white throughout the length of the body.

The average length is about two feet. He is the diameter of a broomstick. The head and body hardly ever measure over 12 inches. The rest is tail.

This lizard has teeth but is not prone to bite. If grabbed he will wiggle frantically and sometimes pieces of tail will fly.

His kissing cousin, the eastern glass lizard, looks a lot like him but exhibits a slight difference in color. If you found one in Texas it would be like the joke: What do you call a really intelligent person in College Station? Answer: A visitor! This lizard prefers to burrow and spends much of his time underground. His diet includes insects, spiders, snails, birds' eggs, and small snakes and lizards.

The slender glass lizard makes his home in the eastern fourth of the state.

SNAKE SEX

I felt I should include this chapter in response to a couple of questions that I am frequently asked. After a few looks over the shoulder and nervous fidgeting, someone will whisper "How do they do it?" The bolder of the two questions starts with a loud "How do you tell a boy snake from a girl snake?" Knowing in my heart that they are waiting for me to talk about eye color or shape of tail, they soon drop eyes and change the subject when I say the word "probe!"

If you are thinking that sleazy seduction among slimy snaky serpents is just something that is not discussed in mixed company, you are right. Most people don't know enough about it to include it in the conversation. That's understandable.

All snake collectors justify their keeping snakes in cages by making an effort to have them reproduce in captivity. The product of successful pairings are then released into the wild or traded, sold, or otherwise exchanged for various reasons. All collectors are familiar with a "breeding loan." It is the same as borrowing the bull I suppose. "Have you seen any mating behavior?" he asked. I replied "No, old Brutus stays in one corner and Patti stays in the other corner and they ignore each other." After a long pause he asked, "Have you played any soft music or offered them a cigarette?"

The primal urge to reproduce is just as strong among the snakes as you will find in any other living thing. As we will see, the process is simple and uncomplicated. I was reading my glossary for this book and noticed a couple of words that can be used in this chapter. This would be a good place to bring them up! There is some argument among those concerned about the exact definition of these terms, but for our purposes we will loosely define: oviparous, viviparous, and ovoviviparous. Oviparous means egg laying and not having to depend on the parent for nourishment. Viviparous refers to an animal giving birth to live young and was reserved for warm-blooded animals. Ovoviviparous is a newer term which means the egg forms within the mother and hatches within the mother and the young are born alive, but dependent on the egg or yolk mass, not the mother, for nourishment. Each of these terms ran into difficulty as new information became known. For our purposes we will say that the large majority of Texas snakes are oviparous, egg layers, and the others are viviparous, giving birth to live young.

Which came first, the snake or the egg? I'm still worrying about a tree falling in the woods! Ah, the egg. The eggs are oval shaped. The shell is leathery and not hard. The eggs are buried in the earth or any other soft substrate that the mother snake can push to one side without much difficulty. She seeks out rotten stumps, hollow logs, sawdust, leaf litter, and manure piles and just generally under stuff. The number of eggs laid depends on the species doing the laying. The numbers range from one to one hundred and four.

When the eggs are laid they are covered with a fluid. When the fluid dries it sticks the eggs together. When you find a "ball" of eggs while digging in the flower bed you can almost be sure that there has been a snake in the area. The eggs will lay under the stuff from 40 to 90 days before they hatch. The young snakes are born with everything they will ever have to take care of themselves and the parents are long gone.

And now for a little anatomy lesson and then along to sex determination. The male snake actually has two penises collectively called hemipenes. These are cylindrical hollow bodies that retract into cavities on either side of the anus. I use the comparison of the finger of a rubber glove. When you remove it from your hand the finger will turn inside out. When one or the other of the hemipenes, never both, is in use it will extend in the same manner. The inner surface becoming the outer surface. Variations in the texture of this surface have been used to identify certain genera of snakes. Just imagine, "By our hemipenes we are known!"

Hemipenis

Milk snake

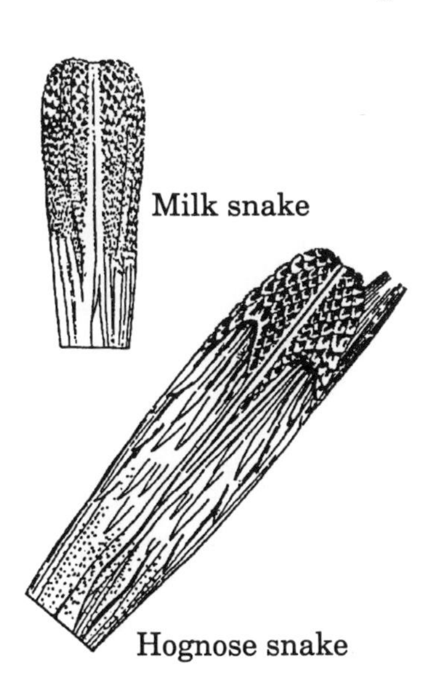

Hognose snake

Texas lyre snake

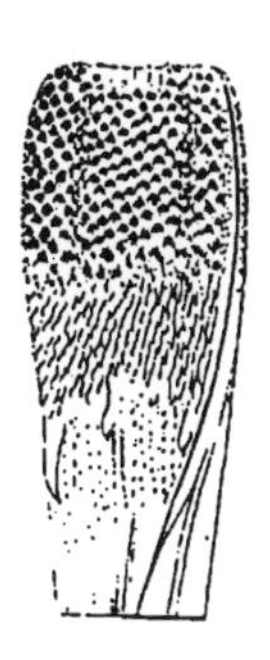

Coachwhip

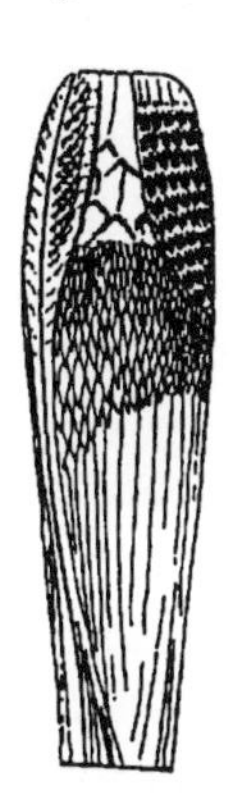

Great Plains rat snake

How does one determine the sex of a snake? How does one locate someone who cares? I can answer the first question, the second is a little more difficult. I would like to say that I have had very specialized training in snake sexing under the guidance of trained veterinarians or professional herpetologists. I would like to say that but it would not be true. Herpetologists don't want you to know and veterinarians don't receive that training in vet school.

I now own a very elaborate set of surgical instruments called "sexing probes." They come in a very attractive leather and canvas pouch and cost over $80.00! I learned the technique by watching a friend of mine at the zoo. The probes are slim, stainless steel rods that have a round ball tip and they come in six sizes. The round ball at the tip prevents an overzealous sexer from inadvertently turning a female snake into a male snake! (oooh!) Use you imagination here.

My first tools for snake sexing were very primitive. I used the hairpin, or more correctly called the bobby pin. These have a blob of hard glue at the tip. This keeps you from stabbing yourself in the hand. These pins come in two sizes, small and large. If straightened out these pins become a poor man's "SNAKE SEXING PROBES."

Here is the procedure. You need two people and one snake. The holder is responsible for controlling the head of the snake. This is important because at the time of insertion a snake does not possess the tact and diplomacy of a human who has assumed the position in the proctologist's office.

The "prober" then turns the tail of the snake over so that the end is pointing toward him and held anus side up. The appropriate sized probe, which has been sterilized and lubricated, is then inserted into the anus of the "probee."

Bear with me now. The ball of the probe is then inserted under the scale that covers the anus. The probe shaft is then inverted and the tip is then (gently) moved down toward the tail tip. If the shaft enters a certain distance it is a male. If the ball stops at the cloaca, it is a girl. That was easy, don't you think?

Drawings on this page by John Hunter
(David Howard, my main man, was too embarrassed!)

Soft music, warm lights, fireplace, beds, rugs, and/or mirrors have no place in the sneaky snake world. When the hormones hit the horny, there are just two factors in the plan; one male snake and one female snake. The male finds the female, a trick discussed in RATTLESNAKE ROMANCE later in this book, and begins to crawl along her back. He is jockeying for position to get his tail beneath and lined up with her tail. He then inserts one or the other of his hemipenes into her cloaca. Never both. Copulation then takes place. The two may remain entwined for hours at a time.

At times the male may capture the female by seizing her neck in his jaws. He usually does not hold on long. It was once thought that an elaborate courtship dance took place before mating. Scientists now believe this act may be only a ritualistic combat dance between two males. Was it good for you?

THE SHED

My two-hundred-pound Burmese python and I were appearing at a furniture store grand opening. I had her seventeen-foot body stretched out on a stack of oriental rugs. She rubbed the skin off around her mouth and began her shedding procedure. I put my hands around her neck and she began to crawl out of the old skin. The crowd grew larger. From a group at the back the chant began. "Push!" "Breathe!" "Push!"

Snakes shed their outer skins periodically and it's a big deal.

Homeowners, campers, hunters and some others who come upon a snake shed consider it a harbinger of certain disaster lurking just around the corner. I once had a family — mom, dad, and two small children — move out of their house and into a hotel after discovering a snake shed hanging across the rafters in the attic. I went to the house, looked around, pronounced the snake gone, and the family returned.

The outer skin, or coat of the snake, takes the form of a wrapper that looks something like cellophane. This "wrapper" is sloughed off as the snake grows larger and as a new surface forms on the scales below. As if you care, you can always tell when a snake is about to shed. His eyes take on the appearance of a fog-bank that has suddenly moved in, and the skin becomes a bluish-opaque. This appearance stays with the snake for four to five days, and during this time, he is for all practical purposes blind. The ordinary snake behavior is to hole up somewhere until the skin is shed before moving around looking for food or mates.

The snake sheds his skin wrong side out. He simply rubs an edge loose around his mouth, snags it on a convenient rock, log, or other rough edge, and crawls out of it. Shedding is an accomplishment of growth and health. It is also dependent on temperature, humidity, time of year, and age of snake — the young snakes shedding more often than the old snakes. This long piece of onion-skin-like, brittle material will usually be longer than the snake it came from. The next time you see a snake shed lying about, rest assured that its former occupant was on the move at the time and is most likely still at it!

PART II
The Rattlesnakes

INTRODUCTION

When I am at least one-hundred miles from home and can qualify as an expert, I am often asked for advice as to what to do in case of an encounter with a rattlesnake. Most people, being people, will do what comes naturally. Then they run like hell! Well, here it is in a nutshell. If you see or hear a rattlesnake, you should stop, look, and listen. If you can tell where the sound is coming from or you can see the snake, you are safe. Simply turn slowly and walk the opposite direction. The snake is attracted by sudden movement or noises that really shake the air. They may also be offended by rough language or strange smells so be calm. Continue to walk slowly until you are out of harm's way and don't go back. People are usually bitten because they do something dumb like get a stick and go back to do battle with the snake. If you don't like your buddies, you can always gather them up and all of you can go back and torment the snake.

People have also been wounded by friendly gunfire when firing blindly trying to hit the snake in the same place seen on television westerns. If you can't hit the side of a barn even if you are locked up in it, how do you expect to hit a target no larger than a golfball!

Rattlesnakes are our most radical reptiles. Of course our Texas rattlesnakes are the biggest, nastiest, and orneriest snakes in the whole world. As we will see they are useful in a number of ways. They are the basis of most of the "snake that almost bit me!" stories. They are good in horror movies. They have been known to strike fear in the hearts of many a yankee planning to travel to Texas.

Rattlesnakes are true reptiles and therefore exhibit all the characteristics. They are covered with dry rough scales. There is no hint of slime or moisture to be found anywhere. The scales on the sides and top are all about the same size. The belly scales are long and thin and look something like the treads on a Caterpillar tractor track. The edges of these belly scales can catch on to the slightest rough surface and allows the snake to crawl and climb with alarming speed. The scale covering is much like wearing a body cast made of millions of fingernails arranged side by side and end to end. These scales protect the rattlesnake from a lot of the brush and barbs of life in the dry arid scrub country. The scales also prevent loss of body moisture that allows him to go without water over an extended period of time.

As in all reptiles the rattlesnake must shed his scales periodically as he grows. The shedding frequency is determined by the amount of food he eats, the surrounding temperature, and the rate of growth. The onset of shedding is signified by the lenses over his eyes becoming cloudy. During this time he is blind and will hole up so as not to encounter an enemy. If I were to try to imagine how he feels, I suppose it would be something like wearing panty hose that are too tight. Or, remember that when you sometimes dress in haste you grab that one pair of underwear that is a little too tight and you have to live with it all day! After a day or two the eye caps will clear and then a day or two later the shedding will take place. The rattlesnake will rub his mouth against a rock or log and the skin will loosen around his lip. The snake then crawls through the rocks and brush until he snags the skin on a rough edge. The old skin comes off inside out and a good ol' boy finds it and tells the story of how his rifle shot missed the snake but it scared him clean out of his skin!

Most snakes lay eggs. They are called oviparous. Some snakes retain the eggs inside where they hatch and the babies are born alive. Rattlesnakes give birth to live babies, and as soon as they are out of the hatch they are ready to put a wrinkle in your doubleknits! The babies are small and seem thoroughly hissed because they go into their coiling, hissing, and striking act at the drop of a gimme cap. The babies have the same venom as mom and in the same strength. They are only less dangerous because they have less of it.

Texas rattlesnakes normally mate in the spring soon after coming out of hibernation. The young are born between August and early October. The actual cycle is difficult to define because the female is capable of storing sperm for a considerable time. Although rare, a mating may not even be necessary to produce a brood.

Rattlesnakes are cold-blooded. You think that is a personality trait but it actually has to do with their body temperature. His optimum body temperature of 85° to 90° F is satisfied by moving to a place where he can find that temperature. If he is too cold he can't digest his food properly and his muscles don't work well. Being too hot is also uncomfy so he is always on the move to find his T-spot!

You know that if you don't like the weather in Texas you just have to wait a minute. Well it do get cold as a well digger's butt so rattlesnakes will hibernate. They are not really social animals but when it is time to sleep it off, they gather in large numbers in a common hole. The "den" is "in" and they will stay there until the Texas winter is over. They will come up for a breather during one of our Indian summers just to sun themselves for a while.

In the spring they emerge from the hole thirsty, hungry, and horny. Then they are off to satisfy those needs not necessarily in that order.

Rattlesnakes eat warm-blooded animals such as birds and mammals. Baby rattlesnakes cannot handle such large food so they will consume insects, small lizards, and frogs. They come by the term "sneaky" because if they were not they would starve to death. Almost all of their prey is faster than they are. The whole process is a marvel to behold and I don't think you would ever hang around long enough to watch so I will describe it as best I can. The rattlesnake hunts whenever it is hungry and the temperature is not too high. He uses his sense of smell, his eyesight, his sensitivity to vibration, and two cute little holes in his face. These little holes are located one on each side of his head between his nostril and his eye. They are so heat sensitive that he can follow a trail left by a mouse as he walks across the ground. The rattlesnake is constantly on the move and he will zero in on whatever is potentially din-din. His criteria is met by motion, size, and body temperature. If the item meets those requirements, he will strike and envenomate. It is interesting to watch him straighten his mouth and fangs after he lets go. He stretches and maneuvers until all is back in position and his mouth will close straight. As soon as he relocates his prey he then considers smell, appearance, and body covering. I say relocate because the bite does not affect the prey instantly and it usually takes off running. He uses all his senses to follow.

If it smells good, looks good, and feels good, then he will begin the swallowing process. He starts by nuzzling the food item with his nose as if to savor the eventuality of a great meal. It is similar to the behavior observed in a person hovering over a well-prepared steak. He then moves to the nose or beak of the animal and opens wide. The rattlesnake has jaws that are four separate bones attached by stretchy ligaments that allow him to swallow something as much as four times his own body circumference. They are not known to attack javelinas or deer other than in self-defense and really prefer the small stuff.

The swallowing process is accomplished in a clean and orderly fashion. The separate jaw bones will move the tiny teeth in and out of the prey and it gives the appearance of the snake crawling over the food item. When the last of the food disappears over the lip the snake will use his neck muscles and gut waves to move the item down to his stomach. He will sport an unsightly lump for a couple of days before the food is completely digested. He will find a warm hiding place while this is going on.

The rattlesnake is an aggressive animal that only wants to be left alone. You bought this book so I assume you want nothing more than to let him have his way. Keep in mind that most snake bites occur because you were not using your head when moving through rattlesnake habitat.

THE RATTLE

They don't call them rattlesnakes because they "rattle" your nerves. Let us take a short trip from the fangs on one end to the buttons on the other end and ponder this marvelous noisemaker; the rattle.

There have been a number of treatises, theses, dissertations, and even position papers on the subject of rattlesnake rattles. Let us turn toward being practical and answer questions for the concrete jungle population. What is it? Where did it come from? Why do they have it? When do they use it? I'll give three out of four of those questions a shot!

The rattle is that thing at the end of a rattlesnake's tail that makes a noise when he vibrates it. Wouldn't it be nice if things could be that simple and answer the question at the same time? The answer to that is "nope!" The complete, tail-end appendage is called the rattle. The individual parts of the rattle are called segments. Each segment is divided into lobes. The segment joining the rattle to the tail of the rattlesnake is known as the attached segment. Do you feel as if you are studying to be a contestant on "Jeopardy"? The oldest segment is the one on the tip which is called the button. The rattle is made of a substance called keratin. As the lobes form at the tail base there is one scale-like piece that becomes detached as the segment matures. That is where the baby rattle sound comes from.

Early thoughts about the origin of the rattle concerned some divine effort to warn unsuspecting creatures of the presence of this nasty snake. If that were the case the rattlesnake would surely starve to death. He would scare off dinner!

There are thoughts that the rattle may have developed because this snake lived in the same habitat and in close proximity to the bison. The noise prevented the snake from getting stomped. This theory is a bit touchy because there have never been fossil remains of rattlesnakes found anywhere near those of the bison. Now that I think about it, that sounds like evidence that it worked!

Most of those who care generally agree that the rattle developed as a specialization of a common reaction in snake behavior. A lot of different species of snakes, both poisonous and nonpoisonous, vibrate their tails when angered or annoyed.

It's kinda like you shake when you get really scared. After reading far too much on the subject I can only say that we don't really know!

Most of the theories concerning the purpose of the rattle have to do with the effect that the noise might have on potential prey. Going back to periods after the Civil War when people suddenly found time on their hands we find these:

- The potential meal would be charmed with sweet sounds.
- The rattle would get the attention of the prey and draw it within range of the evil eye and thereby becoming paralyzed with the power of fascination.
- The food item would become frozen with fright or just scare the soon-to-be din-din into immobility.
- Curiosity killed the cat so perhaps the noise of the rattle would attract the prey within striking range.
- The rattle noise might be mistaken for the sound of a cicada or other insect and the prey might seek out and investigate.
- Use your imagination here and tell yourself the rattling sound might mimic the sound made by running water.
- The sound might be a warning so that the prey could make his escape! Yeh! Right!

Scientists have gone to great lengths to disprove all of these timeworn theories. Again, almost all those herpetologists who care agree that the sound of the rattle is meant to be a warning. It is not a warning aimed at prey. It is not a message to the intruder that "if you keep coming you'll be in deep stuff!" Rattlesnakes and I are somewhat similar on that issue. We are too primitive of mind to have an opinion! It is a warning or threat to any intruder that might cause harm to the snake.

It seems odd to me that people who are afraid of snakes believe them to be deaf, dumb, and blind. Would you react the same way to a charging rhinoceros as you would a sudden confrontation with a Big Mac and fries?

FEAR OF RATTLESNAKES

Over the millenniums the fear of rattlesnakes has been capitalized upon by everyone from grade school children to hunters, trappers, and those other earthy types. There are a million stories out there in the world but I will limit myself to personal knowledge, which has a severe limiting ability.

There is a company somewhere in California called "Rent-a-rattler" and you can rent a rattlesnake for your home or business to act as a security guard. The sign alone should be enough to deter any would-be ne're-do-well. I guess I am guilty of some of this exploitation because there are signs on the windows of my nature center building. One sign reads, "CAUTION, THIS AREA PATROLLED AT NIGHT BY LIVE SNAKES!" Of course if there are any snakes loose, it is not on purpose.

There are cases on the police blotter where people have been charged with assault with a deadly weapon because of snakes. A man in Louisiana was charged, tried, and convicted because he placed a rattlesnake in the mailbox of a business partner to get even with him for a bad business deal. Fortunately, the man looked at his mail before he picked it up. Another man was arrested for putting a rattlesnake in his buddy's pickup truck cab. The snake bit the man and the guy had to pay enormous medical bills.

As I mentioned before, I have hundreds of stories that are snake related. But I've chosen just two as examples of how the old adage "It can't hurt you, but it might make you hurt yourself" seems true to life.

During my former life, and previous occupation, I became acquainted with one of those people that you can readily identify with. He was one of those people who wanted to be able to tell his friends that he had experienced just about everything. If I had said to him that I had just finished parachuting from a plane he would say that he enjoyed each of his ten jumps equally well. It became known around the office that in my spare time I liked to go snake hunting. As soon as old George (not his real name, HA!) found out, he decided that this was an experience he just had to have. He asked very politely if he could accompany me on one of my weekend jaunts into the countryside in search of sneaky, slithery serpents. I reluctantly said yes and we decided on a meeting place. At the appointed time, in a rock-strewn crossroads deep in the countryside, I pulled up in my Toyota. He arrived in his GMC, 4 x 4, sport-wheeled, heavy-duty, more-cubic-inch-motored-than-you-could-imagine pickup. He got my attention the instant his foot touched the ground. He stepped out of the monster truck and stood like a gladiator about to go into battle.

My description here may lose a lot, but try to imagine. I don't remember telling him to bring any particular equipment, so I could best describe his looks as "snake buster!" He had on brand-new roper boots. On his shins, there was something that looked like baseball catcher's shin guards. Hanging from his belt were no less than five pillowcases making him look somewhat like a ballet dancer with gland trouble. His tutu was too-too! From the truck seat, he brought out a black leather case. He laid it on the custom-made truck bed canopy and opened it up. At this point, he reminded me of a pool hustler. He removed three pieces of aluminum shaft and meticulously screwed them together, creating the darndest snake stick I had yet seen. He told me he had purchased this equipment a few days before and was advised this is the ultimate in snake-hunting paraphernalia. Good ol' George was six feet six and weighed somewhere close to the same as a small bull. Therefore, I did not smile, I simply said "Let's go."

"Hanging from his belt were no less than five pillowcases making him look somewhat like a ballet dancer with gland trouble!"

We meandered down a rather tight trail among boulders, large rocks, and rather large trees. He was following me, clanking like some large medieval knight. His gimme cap was on backwards, almost as if to make all the wildlife think he was going the other way! I was surveying the ground, watching for any movement that might indicate our quarry. I spotted a juvenile western diamondback rattlesnake coiled on a flat rock in a spot of sunlight that was filtering down through the leafy canopy above! I stopped and George bumped into me. His reaction was "What?!" I put finger to lip and simply pointed to the point of piled snake. George leaned forward a bit, looked back at me and said, "What?!" I want to make a comment here about George's extensive vocabulary, but we'll just leave it. I pointed at the snake one more time and this time he elaborated and said, "I don't see anything." I pointed my finger as close as I'm going to get it to a rattlesnake and good ol' six-foot-plus-tall George leaned way over. At that instant, he saw the snake. At the same instant, the snake saw George. The snake rattled and George (I really didn't see him do this) somehow turned completely around in midair and hit the ground running at top speed! Unknown to George, we had circled a tree that now stood directly behind us.

Try to imagine the sound of your hand slapping a big chunk of wet liver! That's the sound George made as he bounced off the tree! He fell like a mighty oak and for at least thirty seconds he was out colder than a mackerel. I didn't have time to laugh before he opened his eyes and immediately said, "What?!"

As a nature center director for a number of years, I have gained the reputation of being the one to call when there is any sort of animal mishap in the area. I get snake calls very often and as is the case most of the time when I arrive, the animal has long since disappeared. One such call I remember a frantic voice on the telephone was saying, "There's a rattlesnake coiled by the foundation of my house, and I'm afraid he's going to hurt someone." I told her I would be there very shortly because the address was only three blocks from where I happened to be. I grabbed my snake stick and a bucket and left briskly. I pulled over to the curb in front of the address and witnessed a tense drama that focused at the side of the house. There were no less than six people forming a semicircle. The gardener-looking guy in the center was standing with a garden hoe at port arms and appeared to be protecting the populace! I hurried over to the spot and looked carefully at their point of terror. There, in a tight coil, at the edge of the foundation, was a three-foot long, terrified, coiled and hissing, tail vibrating, harmless rat snake! I smiled and strolled forward, reached over, and picked up the snake. I turned around and found myself suddenly alone. I waited for a short period and the gardener with the hoe appeared around the edge of a hedge. His confidence gathered as he watched me playfully handle the snake. His courage grew as he walked closer. I explained the instinctual defensive behavior of this harmless, rodent-eating reptile, and as I talked, the crowd grew. All were satisfied that they were safe, but I was still asked to remove the big bad snake!

One more phone call and then I'll believe my point has been made. The man on the phone said that he had found a baby rattlesnake under a pile of wood in his backyard. He said he had caught the snake and he would like to bring it to me. I told him to bring it on, but be very careful as rattlesnakes were poisonous and could be dangerous. He arrived at the door along with his wife and three children. I wish you could close your eyes here to envision the sight, but then that wouldn't work because you couldn't read the rest of the story! The man had a full-size leaf rake with a minnow bucket suspended on the prongs. The minnow bucket was covered with a piece of screen wire secured by a twice-wrapped, industrial strength, bungee cord. He said, "It's in here" at which point he sat it on the floor and backed up. His wife and children all stepped back simultaneously. I carefully unwrapped the lid; I then popped it open and looked inside. There lay a small, harmless hognose snake and when he saw me, he went into his "cobra act." You see, when you frighten a hognose snake, they flatten their bodies, raise their heads, hiss loudly, and strike. Their flattened body in the neck region takes on the appearance of an upset cobra. In certain parts of the country they are referred to as spreadin' adders. I reached in and picked up the snake, and we had a duplicate scenario as with the gardener and his hoe. The group had disappeared. Again after a period of time, the man peered through the door and again I began to impart the information. People do the darndest things.

RATTLESNAKE MYTHS

"Sonny, don't ever believe anything you hear and only half of what you see!" My grandaddy's words ring in my ears during almost every conversation dealing with snakes. There are almost as many tall tales, or maybe that should be long tales, about snakes as there are people who talk about them. I have been forced to edit severely in order to get this into one section because there are enough stories for another book.

Let us begin with the assumption that rattlesnakes always rattle before they strike. Scientists now believe that it is more an indication of fright or alarm. If you read the chapter about the rattle you know this already! If in fact it were a warning, they might sound off in the presence of prey and if you have a habit of eating fast food (I'm not talking Big Macs; I'm talking fleet-afoot prey animals), you don't want to frighten them off with a loud noise. The rattlesnake doesn't know how much racket he's making because he literally can't hear himself rattle! I have captured a number of rattlesnakes of various sizes that lack a rattle altogether. They sometimes break off during the shedding process, and as a snake travels through his habitat he might hang a rattle on a branch or on a crack of a rock. I have also captured snakes that have all their rattles and don't seem to be upset enough to make a sound.

Grandaddy always said that you can't even get near a rattlesnake because he can jump "clean off the ground" when he strikes. Tests have shown that a rattlesnake's striking distance is determined by a number of factors. The length of the snake would certainly indicate his striking distance. On a good day, the rattlesnake can strike to a distance of about one-half his total body length. That distance can be affected by such things as the surface on which he lays, which means gravel, sand, leaves, or slope. The air temperature can affect the overall total operation of muscles in that when it's cold, the snake strike would be less than maximum because the animal is cold-blooded and becomes lethargic when cooled. The warmer the temperature, the more effective and lengthy his strike.

I think that one of the reasons I never even thought of killing a snake in my youth was because of a common folk tale. I had always heard that if you kill a snake, his travelling companion would hunt you down and get revenge. You will find rattlesnakes in pairs or groups in only two situations: during periods of mating behavior and during hibernation. Rattlesnakes are primitive animals and to my knowledge are not capable of anything so sophisticated as revenge! They are your basic solitary animal and don't actively seek or require any companionship or assistance with anything.

From East Texas we have a testimony as to the mortality of the rattlesnake. You can chop a rattlesnake into a hundred pieces but he will not die until the sun goes down. The rattlesnake has what can best be described as a primitive nervous system, but even at that, there are lingering nerve reactions in the form of jerks and twists and muscle spasms even after the animal is what we term "legally dead." There have been cases of actual envenomation from the severed head of a rattlesnake from a few minutes to an hour after he lost it! Trust me, a whacked up snake is a dead snake!

Movie makers seem to love snakes because of their supposedly amazing powers. As the story is told, a rattlesnake can hypnotize an animal he plans to eat.

It was hot, windless, humid, wet, and sticky over a large tract of East Texas piney woods. I was trucking along in my usual snake gathering outfit when I noticed some movement across a pile of leaves that covered a fallen branch. It was a bullsnake. He was five feet, six inches long and about the circumference of a golf ball. I crouched slowly and watched carefully. It was obvious from the slow-motion slithering that the bullsnake was on track and prey was at hand. About ten feet in front of the snake's nose there was a small mouse doing little mousey things in the leaves. Mousey things include paw licking, nose rubbing, chest scratching, ear flicking, and munching on a leaf or stem or two. These are much the same things a man does while sitting on the couch watching a football game. The mouse had not spotted me, nor did he have any idea of the impending danger. The bullsnake inched slowly forward (notice the tension building here). The mouse continued to do mousey things, and as the snake neared he slowed his pace accordingly. The nearer he got to the mouse, the more slowly he moved. He came within about a foot and the snake's head stopped in midair, suspended about two inches from the leaf surface. The mouse continued to nibble leaves and do other mousey stuff. The snake's body began to slowly gather behind his statue-like head and his perpetual snakey stare. The moment was at hand! The mouse suddenly looked up from his nibbling, looked at the snake, and in a matter-of-fact way just scampered off and stopped a few yards away. The facial expression on the snake did not, because it cannot, change. I could not resist waxing anthropomorphic and thinking for the snake, "oh shoot!" Maybe I did not think of just those words but you get the picture. The bullsnake then began the process all over again. This time the mouse was watching and eventually disappeared into the brush.

Most of the hype concerning rattlesnakes is geared to only one eventual result and that is death of the snake. If given the opportunity, what would you do to a rattlesnake if you were convinced that if he were to bite you, there would only be a few minutes left of your life? First of all, if you should actually die from the venom of a rattlesnake bite here in Texas, there will be a set of extenuating circumstances a mile long. A few are: size of snake, species of snake, size of victim, health of victim, allergic reactions, site of bite, amount of venom injected, availability of medical care, and the list goes on. Case histories have shown deaths to occur usually many hours to many days after the bite but rarely in minutes. Even if you are going to die there is plenty of time! That does not consider heart attack!

There are snakes in other parts of the world that could possibly kill a person in a few minutes. One that comes to mind is the *Parademansia microlepidotus* or better known as the smooth scaled snake. This critter is found only in parts of New South Wales and Queensland, Australia. There is little known about its habits in the wild. Studies have found that the venom discharged from one bite of this snake could kill 125,000 mice! They are also referred to as the "two-step snake" and that is not a dance.

In most encounters with a rattlesnake the age of the snake is not usually a real worry, but I guess you may have heard that you can tell the age of a rattlesnake by counting the number of rattle buttons at the end of his tail. The rattlesnake must shed its skin periodically as do all reptiles. Each shedding produces a new rattle button. The frequency of shedding is determined by age of snake, food supply, temperature, humidity, and some other factors. Time is not one of those factors.

I can just imagine a campfire out on the plains. The grizzled old cowboys are gathered around and talking to each other. Over to one side of the circle there is the new guy. Loosely referred to as the "greenhorn" or "tenderfoot," he is all ears and taking it all in as gospel truth. When shooting a rattler it is not necessary to take careful aim because when the snake sees the bullet coming, he will strike at it and be killed instantly.

There are a lot of theories about how this tale got started and if you've ever had the occasion to shoot a rattlesnake, you were most likely real close to the snake at the time. My grandfather always commented on my marksmanship by telling me that I couldn't hit the side of a barn if I were locked up in it! As far as a rattlesnake being able to strike with such speed as to intercept an oncoming bullet, I don't think so. There have been various studies done measuring the actual speed of the rattlesnake strike. The old timers tried to be truthful and said the snake could strike faster than the eye could follow. That of course, depends on the age and condition of the eye!

"When shooting a rattler it is not necessary to take careful aim. The snake, when seeing the bullet coming, will strike at it and be killed instantly!"

The classic myth that is even retold by city slickers is the old rope trick. A rattlesnake will not cross a horsehair rope that has been laid out to encircle a bed roll or campsite.

The protective horsehair rope has lost a lot of its popularity with the horse set because they are too expensive and have been replaced with the ordinary hemp rope. The story goes that the snake will not cross the horsehair rope because the hairs scratch their bellies, causing them to turn away. If you have ever had the occasion to actually examine the scales of a snake, particularly those on his belly, you will find that they are much the same consistency as your fingernail. As a matter of fact, snake scales are made up of the same substance as the human fingernail. This surface could in no way be affected by something as weak and frail as a hair from a horse. I have watched many times when rattlesnakes crawl through dense briar and even over prickly pear cactus and barrel cactus with no change in direction or even a flinch. This was even when the snake was not alarmed and not being pursued. Early studies have tried to test the rope hypothesis and they have found that, regardless of the type of rope, it was certainly no deterrent to the snake. One might read about cowboys who have put the rope around the bedroll, waking up to find several snakes on the perimeter as if waiting for the gate to open. Another story involves using a striped black and white rope that would make it look like a king snake! And as we all know, a king snake will eat a rattlesnake. There are some who believe that snakes might be repelled by the human odor one might find on a rope. I think there may be market for an item I have been developing through the years; I want to call it "Snake Away." It might be considered very simple, yet could be effective. It consists of a small, shiny, smooth, round river rock that one must carry on his person at all times. The mere presence of this rock would prevent the merciless attack of almost any rattlesnake!

"The mere presence of this rock would prevent the merciless attack of almost any rattlesnake!"

There are stories about how animals that live with the rattlesnake learn to cope. The roadrunner, upon finding a rattlesnake at rest, will encircle the snake with a fence of cactus pods. The roadrunner then awakens the snake with a fluttering of wings. The irritated snake, in its frustration of not being able to cross the pods, will sink its fangs into itself and die from the poison. Right.

If you have read anything on the preceding pages, you remember that rattlesnakes have no problem crawling across prickly pear cactus. Secondly, the rattlesnake seems to be immune to its own venom. Roadrunners are large birds that eat just about anything, which include reptiles, such as lizards, snakes, and even newly hatched turtles. Scorpions, centipedes, and big hairy tarantulas are consumed with great joy. I have watched the roadrunner kill a nonpoisonous rat snake, and his method in no way involved cactus. The rat snake in question coiled and began striking as is his instinctual urge. The roadrunner charged in and out, delivering lethal pecks with his long beak. He persisted, the snake resisted, and all life ceased and desisted!

Upon an informal survey of family, friends, colleagues, and total strangers these stories seem to be the most popular.

SIZE WISE

As you well know, the discussion of almost any topic between two Texans will almost always come around to size. With rattlesnakes that information is more meaningful than just "yarn enhancement!" The size of a rattlesnake will determine the distance he can strike, the length of his fangs, and the amount of venom he has to produce misery. It is also important in determining who told the best story. The size range in Texas rattlesnakes goes from less than two feet in the pygmy rattlesnake to over six feet in the diamondback. That does not take into consideration the one that almost bit you which I am sure was over fifteen feet long and as big around as your upper leg!

The only reliable way to measure a rattlesnake is while he is alive. A measurement made of the skin is useless because it will stretch from inches to feet. The next closest you can be in measurement is to put the tape to a freshly killed snake. This will be difficult, because when a Texan kills a rattlesnake you have to take the lengths of several pieces and add them up!

So how big is the biggest rattlesnake? It is difficult to determine the difference between an obvious tall tale and anything to be considered an accurate measurement. There are a number of Texas story tellers who put their snake stories in print so long ago that they have become accepted as fact through simple persistance. Campfire stories from hunters and cowboys trying to scare the beejeebies out of a tenderfoot have told of 10-to 20-foot rattlers. The largest Texas rattlesnake is undoubtedly the western diamondback. After condensing as many reports as I cared to read I have come to a "somewhere around" measurement of 7 feet

4 inches from tip of nose to the base of the rattle. At the risk of uttering blasphemy I will say that the largest rattlesnake in the United States does not live in Texas. The eastern diamondback of Florida and thereabouts grows to a length of eight feet.

I should also mention that people now outnumber the rattlesnake population and that has an effect on their size range. The rattlers don't live as long as they used to. They don't have the food availability they once had. When we consider the old accounts of size it may just be that they were bigger then. Well, that was then and this is now. Don't look for monsters.

RATTLESNAKE POISON

The scientific types are still not sure why rattlesnakes have venom in the first place. Millions of years seem to have changed a mild saliva, much like the digestive juice in your mouth, into a substance that to this day has not been completely figured out. It doesn't seem to be something forced upon them by the struggle to survive. If that were the case why didn't all the snakes have poison?

I know how we all enjoy listening to Uncle Joe or Brother Bob tell his personal experience stories, and I know that there are times when you'd just as soon go to the bathroom and come back when the story is over. I have a nephew who attempted to solve that problem at one of my great family gathering speeches. He listened patiently for quite some time and then without much fanfare, he reached into his pocket, withdrew a quarter, tossed it to me, and said, "Why don't you go call somebody who cares?"

Anyway, back when I was younger and smarter, I did a particular snake presentation for classroom audiences that I simply labeled "Poisonous Snakes of Texas." I'll describe the scene for no other reason but that it was a lot of fun at the time. When time came for my particular show, I constructed a snake pit in the center of the classroom. It consisted simply of four 4x8 sheets of 3/4 inch plywood (I love this technical talk!) nailed together at the corners forming a box. I placed two-by-four poles in each corner that extended up four feet above the edge of the plywood. I then wrapped the entire kit-and-caboodle in chicken wire and, with a wave of my arms, declared the whole thing "SAFE!"

The snakes I used for my presentation were stored in "Venomous Snake Boxes" which were of my own ingenious design. Actually, I got the idea from numerous animal containers that have double doors. I cheated a bit with the snakes because as you and I both know, when a reptile gets cold, he becomes somewhat lethargic. To accomplish this, I simply stored my coral snake, copperhead, water moccasin, and rattlesnake in the refrigerator for a couple of hours before the show!

On one particular class day, I found myself in somewhat of a hurry, so the "cooling off period" for the snakes was not as long as it should have been. I had a double class that day which consisted of sixty students, so there was quite a crowd gathered around the box. I had waxed eloquent about the first three poisonous snakes and my big diamondback rattlesnake was next on stage. While talking continuously, I unlocked the ominous looking wooden box and deftly opened the first door with my snake stick. The inner door consisted of a frame covered with screen wire. I leaned forward to check on the position of the rattlesnake and he took his cue! With remarkable force, his open mouthed, extended fanged head hit the screen wire with such force that the door jumped.

I suddenly felt what I thought was someone playing a trick with a water gun right in my face. One of my eyes began to burn, and I realized what had happened. The big rattlesnake had decided to play the role of an African spitting cobra and I caught the spray. Needless to say, the inside doors of my snake boxes are now covered with one-quarter-inch Plexiglas.

You are obviously still reading, so that one must have been a hit. I'll tell you another one. Charlie the western diamondback rattlesnake was for years my favorite presentation animal, the main reason being he had undergone two operations which rendered him basically harmless. He still had his nasty attitude which goes along with being a western diamondback rattlesnake, but he didn't know he shot blanks!

To continue, I took Charlie to a high school assembly because the program theme was Texas Cowboys. I think they wanted me to put a cowboy boot and foot across his neck and threaten him with a large knife, but I would have no part of that. They had to be content with my snake handling techniques and more information than they really needed to know about rattlesnakes. I deftly pinned old Charlie's head to the floor with my snake stick and picked him up using the most advanced and acceptable venomous snake handling techniques. As I held him aloft showing his nasty (though useless) fangs, suddenly, one of the fangs pressed down against the bottom of his throat. It continued through the skin and came back into my thumb! For a split second, I waited for my thumb to become a multicolored balloon, but then I realized I just had a pinprick in my phalange. Needless to say, I no longer pin down large venomous snakes.

There's a thing about venom which makes it complicated, so I have to rewrite it as I go along and when I understand what I am saying I'll let you know. Over a period of millions of years or more than you could imagine, some snakes manufactured a poison different from that of the other snakes and have different effects. One poison works on the nerves, and the other on the blood. The makers of the nerve poison include the snakes like the mambas, cobras, and our local beauty the coral snake. Their venom is called neurotoxic.

Most of our Texas rattlesnakes manufacture the blood poison which is known as hemolytic. Both poisons are bad news, but by far the nastiest one is the blood poison. It is said by those who care that the nerve poison is the more primitive of the two. And so the blood poison is a newer and better product. By the way, the nerve poison acts much faster and does its nasty stuff far more quickly than the blood poison. That means absolutely nothing to the snakes because they did not acquire it for use against man, but instead, to kill prey.

It also happens that the two poisons are rarely pure. That is to say, the nerve poison of the cobra usually has a trace of blood poison and our rattlesnakes have some nerve poison. When you're lying on your back staring up at the blue sky, your skin changing colors, and you're giving serious thoughts to your will, it doesn't seem to matter much. I'm going to give you a thumbnail sketch of what these poisons might do to you. Rumor has it that any snake in Africa that bites you, you get to take about two steps and then you're dead. It's not quite that simple. The venom, no matter which kind, will react on each individual in a different manner. The circumstances involved are fodder for another complete book!

When striking the prey animal, the most venomous snake hangs on for a moment while its fangs deliver a prescribed dose into the critter. This rarely happens with a man because the snake most likely inflicts his "get-away-from-me" bite, and the man's immediate reaction is to yank the snake off. On being bitten by a snake possessing neurotoxic poison such as a cobra, the usual symptoms are pain, weakness in the legs, and drooling. I have observed grown men doing that when looking at a perfectly cooked Texas T-bone. Those symptoms occur simply because paralysis sets in on the muscles of the mouth. The tongue too becomes paralyzed and the victim, although able to hear, doesn't talk very often. He begins to vomit and has difficulty breathing. That is because the paralysis has affected his diaphragm and the lungs aren't working properly. What happens is this: when the poison is injected, it is distributed by the blood and attacks the nerve cells and the nerve centers. Finally, it paralyzes the nerve center that controls breathing and the lungs collapse. Are you having pleasant thoughts?

And now to the poison of most of our good ol' Texas rattlesnakes. They are referred to as pit vipers, the reason being they have small holes or pits located on their heads between their nostrils and their eyes. These pits are thought to be, among other things, heat-sensing structures that allow the animal to track and capture warm-blooded prey. All are venomous but only a few are really deadly. All of those deadly ones don't live in Texas. This hemolytic poison breaks down the blood and destroys its ability to coagulate. The blood vessels, particularly the small capillaries, are also broken down and the destroyed red corpuscles ooze around the surrounding tissues and cause great swelling and discoloration. Internal bleeding also occurs in the stomach, bladder, and the bowels. The skin becomes cold and clammy. The victim begins to vomit and things don't generally go well!

Snake venom is a clear yellow liquid, odorless and tasteless. Finding out that it's tasteless is not something even I would try to ascertain. The fact is that anyone could drink a cupful, provided he did not have a sore in his mouth or an ulcer in his stomach, and suffer no ill effects. Only when injected is it dangerous.

Snake venom will keep for years without losing any of its poisonous properties. Dried venom has been stored for over 30 years and, when dissolved in water, it is found to be as bad news as ever. Poison taken from a dead snake will be just as strong as that taken from a live snake, but not if the snake has begun to, how do we say it, rot!

The formula of snake poison is not known. It has a protein base, but chemical analysis does not tell us all the agents that are present. Most of its many enzymes and peptides are devoted to digestion. The venom reacts in humans the same way it works in prey animals. It simply begins to disintegrate the living tissue. You start to digest!

RATTLESNAKE ROMANCE

The last rays of the sun were disappearing over the edge of the water trough. The light breeze caused the strips of cedar bark on the fence posts to slap and rustle. He sensed a coolness in the air as he slithered nearer the moisture of the water trough. The sand on which he lay was still scorching hot from the leftover Texas sun. His last taste of moisture came from a few drops of dew that he had licked from the lower pods of a big ol' prickly pear cactus. He had not eaten during the weeks he had traveled since he left Durango. He could smell the water and it seemed closer every second. The tank was long and tall. He knew he must find a corner in order for him to climb up and over the top. Just as he approached the sought after angle he became aware of a second scent. She had passed that way and just recently. Of all the lousy abandoned water troughs in West Texas why did she have to come to this one. (I love "Casablanca!")

We will now discuss the when, where, and how of rattlesnake romance. Try to be mature! First we must determine the sex of all parties involved. Pay attention! This could come up at a party. Sexual dimorphism in snakes is a comparative and sometimes matter-of-opinion situation. It seems that each expert uses a different set of characteristics. Most of them are only applicable if you have a number of snakes for comparison. There are some facts however. Generally speaking, female rattlesnakes are shorter than the males. So, is the one at your feet a short boy or a long girl! Do you care?

Snakes, unlike mammals and birds, grow as long as they are alive. Measurements must be taken at a time when the snake is considered an adult so the whole thing is arbitrary. There seem to be some differences in color and pattern between the sexes. These differences vary between species and would not be of any use to the casual observer. The tail length is most likely the best indicator without actually having to touch the snake. The tail of the male is longer and thicker than that of the female and it tapers gradually from the body. The female has an abrupt tapering from the anal opening back. For those of you who are not sure where the snake tail begins this again is of little use.

There is one other theory that could really be a killer. Some say that male rattlesnakes have four fangs and the females have only two. Rattlesnakes shed old fangs or they are broken off after an aggressive encounter with their food. There is always a set or two of reserve fangs in the wings to replace those lost. These "next" fangs are present in both males and females. The only reliable way to determine the sex of a live snake can be summed up in one word, "probe." That is usually enough information for the really uninterested to change the subject. If you skipped the chapter called SNAKE SEX, shame on you! I would suggest you review that section before you press on.

In the vast expanses of the rattlesnake habitat just how do the snakes find each other? Rattlesnakes have scent glands located near their anal opening. These glands produce substances called pheromones. During the mating period, which will vary between species, the female lays a pheromone trail. The male, using his sense of smell, will locate and follow the trail. There are times when two or more males will fall upon the same trail. That is why the fight starts!

The "combat dance" was once thought to occur only during the pursuit of a female. First of all to call what two male rattlesnakes do as "combat" is by no means the case. Neither party is actually harmed by the encounter. The word "dance" doesn't fit when you consider that the two creatures have neither arms nor legs to be much at dancing. This display was first thought to be the actual mating procedure, but further study has shown that only the males participate. It is also now known that the males will do this whether there is a female present or not. They are not out to win any fair maidens. They dance only because they instinctively don't like each other.

Actual snake copulation occurs when the male entwines his body with the female. The anal openings come in contact and mating will proceed. The process may take a few minutes, or in some cases, a few days. The gestation period will vary among species but it is usually about sixty days. The young are then born alive and ready to be rattlesnakes.

THE DEN

I was sitting in my den recently surrounded by my den mates; the family. Notice here how I relate everyday life situations to the topic at hand. Boring isn't it? We were watching a commercial on television. The speaker was the owner of a company that sold tea. He was sitting on a big rock located in a park somewhere in Utah. He was saying that he searched all over the world for tea. That was his business. My son piped in "There's no tea in Utah!" My wife then asked, "How do you spell Utah?" Life is funny without any help.

Every good hunter or trapper is aware of the fact that snakes hibernate. I guess most of the bad ones know that also! Some of the most exciting campfire stories involve the big old "nests" of rattlesnakes. Rattlesnakes are not the only snakes that den and all snakes in temperate regions hibernate. They draw much more attention to themselves because of the vast numbers in one place and the fact that they will come out of the den during a warm day. If you see fifty or so rattlesnakes laying around in one place, you will pay attention!

The denning activity seems to be totally dependent on seasonal temperature change. Here in Texas the den sites are not as elaborate as those in the north because the periods of hibernation are shorter. Sleep is often interrupted by warm spells when the snakes will haul out to enjoy the sun. Our rattlers will take advantage of any hole or rock crevice and in this situation there might only be a few that share the same underground condo.

"Here in Texas, sleep is often interrupted by warm spells and the snake will haul out to enjoy the sun."

The fact that rattlesnakes are reptiles, that they are poikilothermic, ectothermic, or the term we use with in-laws, "cold-blooded," means their muscle action, digestion, and really all behavior is controlled by the climate. Our mild climate determines the length of hibernation and the depth of the hole. A rattlesnake at 40° F. is one immobile, stiff critter. Therefore, he must be in a very protective situation when it gets to where he can't move. Even during active periods in late fall it is not unusual to find a rattlesnake in the cool of the morning that is so lethargic he will strike in slow motion. I have witnessed this action at rattlesnake round-ups where handlers are known to refrigerate the snakes. Then they can play with the frosty critters and lessen their chances of getting nailed.

The jury is still out as to why the same rattlesnakes return to the same den each fall, but they do. It has been suggested that the snakes are territorial and it is just an owner's prerogative. There are some logical advantages to the den. One might be that for those rattlesnakes that mate in the spring it would be easy to find a partner. Safety in numbers might also be a factor. When large numbers of snakes are in close proximity they will communicate by movement when danger threatens and they can dive!

Although they are cold-blooded there may be some advantage in "cuddling" to conserve any heat that might be present. The den could be detrimental in the case of overcrowding in that the last one in might have to leave something hanging out, and get it frozen off!

FIRST AID FOR RATTLESNAKE BITE

In my travels throughout the state while doing presentations about snakes I have always taken along examples of my topic. I keep on hand three of the four venomous kinds of snakes found in Texas. I say three because it is extremely difficult to keep a coral snake alive because of their refusal to eat in captivity. Inevitably someone will ask what they should do if they are walking down a trail or through the woods and they hear the tell-tale sound of a rattlesnake. I tell them that unfortunately the human startle reflex is involuntary. We tend to do what comes naturally, then we run like hell!

I can easily summarize the first aid for rattlesnake bite here in Texas in one sentence.

> IF YOU ARE BITTEN BY A RATTLESNAKE, HAVE SOMEONE TAKE YOU TO A DOCTOR.

Does that sound like I have forgotten something? Is that what John Wayne would do? Is that what your second cousin on your father's side would do? You will notice that I did not mention the tie-cut-suck-spit method nor did I mention the ice bag that keeps your six-pack cold. There is also a syringe-like gizmo that sucks that old poison right out. And, last but not least, you may choose to shock the daylights out of yourself with a stun gun! I will relate a story as told to me by an acquaintance I met while working as a policeman during another life.

This person was a doctor's assistant at a large trauma center hospital. The call came that there was a snakebite victim on the way. Like most metropolitan hospitals, this one had a supply of antivenin on hand for just such occasions. The man came through the double doors on a gurney being pushed by some less-than-enthusiastic paramedics. The man was semiconscious and his arm, which was swollen bigger than a frog in a butter churn, was laying across his chest. At the upper portion of his arm there was a wooden stick laying lengthwise down his arm and each end of the stick was taped around his arm. Around the center of the stick was a piece of electrical cord which disappeared into the flesh of his arm. At the base of his thumb there was a series of slashes which were deep and long but there was no blood. The arm was various shades of black, blue, and green.

The electrical wire was a tourniquet which had been twisted tight with the stick and was held in place by the tape. The doctors went to work to restore the circulation to his arm. They had to quickly stitch the slash wounds so he would not bleed. He regained consciousness whereupon he was questioned about his experience. A snake of unknown species had bitten him on the thumb and he had applied first aid to himself. He was asked to describe the snake. He said it was about two feet long and had stripes running down its back and both sides. This description can only fit a species of garter snake, ribbon snake, or lined snake and a few others that are totally harmless! This story is about third hand so I suspect some of it may suffer from the gossip game influence.

You could lose an arm or leg just by doing the first aid. There are some "Snakebite Kits" on the market that will go a long way in helping you to become an amputee. One of those that can be purchased at any sporting goods or variety store is a compact little oblong rubber green thing that looks like a horse size vitamin pill. It comes apart in the middle and inside you will find all the apparatus needed to have your nickname changed to "lefty!" There is a length of nylon string that must be five-hundred-pound-test trotline string. It won't break! Packed alongside the string you will find a two-inch surgical scalpel blade. Armed with this you are instructed to make two 1/4 inch deep incisions 1/4 inch long in the form of an X over each fang puncture. If you have panicked enough to cut yourself, are you going to take the time to be so precise? No, you will most likely put Jack The Ripper to shame.

Then there are the suction cups. There are instructions printed on the ends! If you squeeze it one way you get "low" suction. If you press it the other way you get "high" suction. If I were convinced that suction was going to save my life, would I be concerned with "low" suction? I think I would want something that would take the chrome off a trailer hitch! The actual suction offered by these cups is not of sufficient strength to suck out anything. The people who manufacture this thing offer a disclaimer for any problems that occur.

Another charming little device looks like a giant plastic hypodermic needle. It comes with four different sized suction cup heads that simply snap on. The theory is that when you are bitten you are to place the suction tip over the fang puncture and pull up on the plunger and the poison just comes right out. There are some other interesting supplies. You get three Band-Aids. There are folded instructions that are arranged like a map of the United States and about as big. You would most likely die before you read all the information! The other tool may need some explanation that is not supplied in the instructions. There is a safety razor! I guess you would want to look good when you go to the doctor. All this comes in a smart looking plastic case with belt loops on the back. You should put it on your hunting belt right beside that Bowie knife that you never use. The jury is still out on this device but so far there has been no significant evidence that it works.

The advice to "slap the ice pack from the six-pack cooler over the fang holes" is out. It is based on the theory that cold will slow the action of the chemical components of the venom. The venom is made up of many different components, and some of them may even be speeded up by adding ice. Common sense will tell you that if you hold ice against your skin for a long time, it will cause problems. Can you say "frostbite?"

You may have heard that you can shock the area of the snakebite and neutralize the venom. There will soon be a number of places you can buy a stun gun for use in case of snakebite. I would suggest that you use it to amuse yourself while on the way to the doctor place. This all got started down in South America. There is some evidence that it works and just as much evidence that it doesn't. So far most of the positive argument comes from testimonials. The way I feel about electrical shock I think I will take my chances with the snake venom!

I feel it necessary here to dance with a bit of folklore because the Indians started it and for some it may still be gospel. Any number of different writers have reported snakebite cures over the years. I have looked to L.M. Klauber, a noted rattlesnake expert, for a synopsis of these remedies. Bind the liver and intestines of the snake in question to the bite. Smash the head of the rattlesnake and apply that to the bite. Swallow the rattlesnake's heart with beer or wine. Bruise the snake's liver and slap it on the fang puncture. How does one bruise a liver? Rub on liberal amounts of rattlesnake oil. I'm sure Judge Roy Bean would have approved. Let the victim bite off the head of the rattlesnake. Grab the snake by the head and tail and take a bite out of the middle. You awake yet? Drink boiled snakeweed in sweet milk. Rub on the saliva from a fasting man. Apply a poultice of melted cheese. And the list seems to be endless.

The one I like best is the split chicken treatment. In this act, a live chicken is split or slit and the bleeding flesh is applied to the snake bite as a poultice. Whereupon, the chicken's meat should turn green or its comb blue as the poison is being drawn out. Then of course you would just use fresh chickens until they no longer turn colors. Needless to say, or maybe necessary to say, that this act does absolutely nothing for the victim. Not only that, you have made a certain number of chickens very dead! I suppose a contemporary application of the old folklore would be to dash to the nearest hamburger joint and order a cheeseburger with double meat and double cheese and first aid yourself!

I reiterate, and I'll say it again also, IF YOU ARE BITTEN BY A RATTLESNAKE IN TEXAS, HAVE SOMEONE TAKE YOU TO A DOCTOR. Stay calm, which is easy to say while sitting here at the word processor, but it is good advice. Don't run wild or climb a tree. Don't try to catch the snake because he will bite you again! Keep your bitten part as motionless as is possible. Take heart! More people die from complications from bee stings than from a snakebite here in Texas.

THE TEXAS TYPES

There are ten species of rattlesnake that are known to live and work in the state of Texas. But, in order to save you some embarrassment when the subject comes up at parties and other social gatherings I will mention the timber rattlesnake. There are some canebrake rattlesnakes that appear in the northeastern part of the state that seem to have some physical characteristics of the out-of-state timber rattlesnake. These may be a crossbreed and not a legitimate representative of the Texan. Keep in mind when you look at the range maps and the boundaries that rattlesnakes can't read, and if you find one in the wrong county, it could happen.

Banded Rock Rattlesnake

This snake occupies a habitat that almost misses the Texas map! You could say that if one leaves the El Paso city limits, you've run out of snake! This one looks a lot like the mottled rock rattlesnake, and most of the snake people think it is the prettiest. I haven't told you what a mottled rock rattlesnake looks like yet but hold on.

The adult snake is a ghostly grey color. He has black bands that cross his body every couple of inches. The adult banded rock rattlesnakes measure around two feet in length. The record length is 32.5 inches (J. Frank Dobie not withstanding!). It seems to be more curious than the other rattlesnakes and will stand its ground even when disturbed. It seems to like to hide and watch. This snake roams around during the day, especially after a rain. It seems to enjoy moisture, and owing to the average rainfall in El Paso it doesn't get out much.

This rattlesnake eats mostly lizards, but like all snakes it will partake of an occasional mouse, bird, or frog. The live-born babies are about seven inches long with a bright pattern and a brilliant yellow tail tip. There are two to five offspring that are born in the spring, tra la!

Black-tailed Rattlesnake

These seem to be the most laid back of the Texas rattlesnakes. They hole up in the most inaccessible places and therefore don't encounter people a whole lot. The jury is still out as to the potency of their venom, but it may not be as bad as that of the western diamondback rattlesnake. Think about that if one bites and you are sitting there watching your arm swell up! This rattler is restricted to the canyons of the Western Edwards Plateau and is likely the most abundant rattlesnake within its range.

I know you may have guessed already, its tail is black! The back is tan, olive, or greyish. His belly is yellow with a green tinge. The adults grow to an average of thirty-two inches. The record length is fifty-two inches. Like one of the legendary people with fangs, this snake only leaves the tomb at night. They seem to like temperatures in the sixties. They have been captured in mid-February so don't go kickin' around in the dark in the winter on the Edwards Plateau.

The adult rattlesnake eats small mammals. The youngsters will eat slow lizards. The babies are born alive, about seven in number, and are around eight to ten inches long.

I was road hunting one night and happened upon one of these snakes straddling the center stripe. I was not particularly interested in a black-tailed rattlesnake so I used my stick to move him off the road. About one hour later I came back that way and he was hugging the center stripe again! Add one thing to this entry; black-tailed rattlesnakes are stupid! You might also consider that there was a grown man driving slowly up and down a deserted road looking for snakes in the middle of the night.

"...........consider a grown man driving back and forth, up and down a country road, in the middle of the night, looking for snakes."

Canebrake Rattlesnake

This one is in the midst of a herpetological controversy. Some think this and the timber rattlesnake are the same species. Some think it is an entirely different species. Some think it is just a separate race divided by geographical space. Some of us sit and think and some of us just sit! You bought this book so I doubt seriously if you really care what "some think!"

The average length canebrake rattlesnake measures 42 to 60 inches long. The record is over seven feet. He makes his home in the swampland and other watery places in the southern half of East Texas.

One of the differences between the timber and the canebrake rattlesnakes is that the canebrake has a neat dark stripe running backward from his eyes. There is a reddish stripe down the middle of his back. This stripe separates the black cross bands along either side of his body. Some timber rattlesnakes have the stripe and some don't. Don't make any bets on the stripe.

The babies are born alive and are real nasty little creatures right out of the hatch! I use hatch figuratively because the babies are born alive. They are strongly patterned but are paler in color. The main color of this snake is a funny shade of brown that could best be described as greyish. That puts a few kinks in my identification system but so does just about everything else!

The canebrake rattlesnake loves frogs and toads but he is not above biting a bird or snatching a rat or two.

Desert Massasauga

These snakes are found by the passel in West Texas from Big Bend to Lubbock and a few scattered through the Valley. He has brown blotches on his back against a creamy brown color and a white belt. The adults average in size less than eighteen inches, with the record specimen only a little over twenty inches.

The desert massasauga only messes around at night and enjoys road hunting for an easy way to find grasshoppers and crickets. Captive snakes seem to develop peculiarities and will eat only one thing on the menu. Some like mammals and some like lizards. Go figure!

The name is a bit misleading in so far as its choice of habitat. He prefers the short grass prairie. There are two litters a year and the live-born young number five to thirteen. The babies are about eight inches long.

Mojave Rattlesnake

The Mojave rattlesnake is probably the most dangerous snake north of Mexico. It has the quickest strike and the venom has the most potency. The venom has been equally compared with the venom of the cobra. It can be found from El Paso through the Big Bend country. Although we haven't discussed these two yet, the front half of the Mojave is colored like the western diamondback and the back half is marked like a prairie rattlesnake. Look at the description under those two, and I won't have to put anything else here. It is a slender snake measuring less than thirty-two inches in length. The record is just over fifty-four inches.

When they notice you, they will lower their heads, raise their tails, and look particularly nasty. They flip their tails from side to side, much like the arm on a metronome. Scary, isn't it? This is a snake of the desert, often found in open brush or grass-covered flats and on mountain slopes.

The Mojave rattlesnake eats mostly rodents and prefers ground squirrels, pocket gophers, and white-footed mice. There have not been many of these born in captivity, so there is not a lot of information about reproduction.

Mottled Rock Rattlesnake

This is a Southwest Texas snake from Big Bend to the Guadalupe National Park. His colors are highly variable and you'll have pink snakes with dark blotches, and little blue snakes with black spots. These bright colors help them hide from their airborne predators and assist in sneaking up on their colored-vision lizard food. They average under two feet, and the record length is 32.5 inches. As the name implies he is a rock-dwelling snake and enjoys rock ledges and bluffs.

These are the less of the nocturnal rattlesnakes and can be found goofing around in the early morning and then again in the early sunset. They are always on the lookout for a lizard not paying attention to where he's going! They will also take in an occasional frog, salamander, or insect, and they're not above consuming another snake. The live-born babies are fewer in number than any of the other Texas rattlesnakes averaging two or three. The babies measure eight to ten inches.

Prairie Rattlesnake

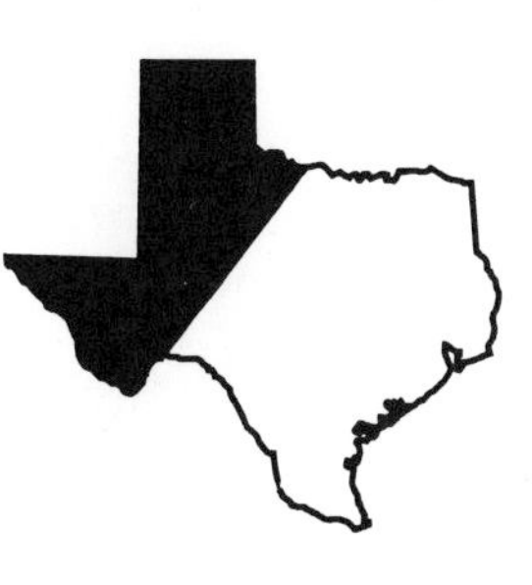

The prairie rattlesnake is found in much of the Panhandle and southward all the way to the Big Bend. They have oval-shaped, brown patches down the center of the back which change to narrow cross bands near the rear end. The belly is yellowish-white. This is a slender pit viper that maxes out just over 4.5 feet, the average being around two feet.

Prairie rattlesnakes like it hot! It enjoys the grasslands of the Great Plains, but in winter, it likes to den in rocky outcroppings. He is known to climb mountains, not just because they are there, but because it's a good place to find food. He preys upon short-sighted prairie dogs and burrowing owls that stay home too much! He will also consume other small mammals and ground nesting birds. The young will eat lizards. The babies are born live and measure eight to eleven inches long.

Timber Rattlesnake

This snake grows to an average length of forty inches and the last record I read was seventy-four inches. He is sometimes called the banded or velvet-tailed rattler. The color combinations vary between yellow-brown to green-grey. This animal is about the only rattlesnake that is found in the Northeast and has disappeared from much of its habitat. This particular rattlesnake doesn't seem to care much about roommates, as he will den with copperheads and other snakes during the winter. As the name implies, this is a snake of wooded areas and is most abundant in the tall grass where the mice and rats play. The live babies are born in late summer and average ten in number.

I am sure this is something that came up at your last party so I will mention it here. There exists a yellow phase and a black phase of this snake. This very noticeable color variation adds to the controversy about the timber rattlesnake and the canebrake rattlesnake being the same snake. The yellow phase has spots along his back plus a row down both sides. Do I really need to explain the black phase?

This snake makes his home in the northeast piney woods of Texas.

Western Diamondback Rattlesnake

This big dude is the biggest, baddest, and the best one. He is the largest and most widespread and most dangerous snake in the state of Texas. Almost all of the serious cases of snakebite treated in Texas hospitals in a year are caused by this snake. Very few people die from diamondback bites because our technology has improved over the last five years. Those who don't make it are usually children and sometimes highly stupid hunters.

They are found just about all over except extreme East Texas. The overall color varies from light grey to almost red. The tail is the most identifiable characteristic because it is boldly black and white banded. It is often called the coon-tailed rattler. The belly is unmarked, yellowish-white. "While I was driving my Dodge pick-me-up truck down an old country road, I seen this snake. His head was on one side of the road and his tail disappeared off the other side. He was as big around as my leg." Although they are not quite that big, they do sometimes measure over 7.5 feet. The adults average three or four feet. The huge ones are not as common as Bubba would like to think. I have discussed Texas-sized snakes in another chapter.

They prefer to hunt during the cooler part of the day and at night. When we get into stories, this rattler is the one we are almost always talking about. He eats mostly warm-blooded prey and mammals seem to be a preference. He is a great control for the rabbit population and also enjoys rats, mice, gophers, and ground squirrels.

The babies are born live around September. There are between nine to fourteen that exit the hatch and they are about ten inches long.

I am sitting here at a back corner table. I am trying to pay attention. "And visiting us from the El Paso club,

George Michaelson." "Hello George!" "From the great city of McKinney, Texas, please welcome........" "Hello........!" I am the program today. For lunch these Rotarians will have baked chicken, potatoes, green beans, apple pie, and half an hour's worth of poisonous snakes. I am watching that marvel of engineering; the door stop. Every few seconds it does a little skip-step and the door closes a little more. I brought Charlie today. He is a five foot long, big around as my arm, foul tempered western diamondback rattlesnake. Skip-step, stutter, skip-step, I hope that door closes soon.

"Today we have Mr. Jim Dunlap of the Plano I.S.D. Living Materials Center, blah, blah!" That dumb door stop finally stopped the door. I usually save Charlie for last. He is big and impressive and very dangerous looking. I will use my aluminum shafted snake hook to swing Charlie from his lock box up onto the table top. He will coil and rattle violently. The front row of business-suited men will move back noticeably. After going over his behavior, habitat, food preference, ecology, and anatomy I will extol the difficulties of getting him back into the box.

Today Charlie was great. As I tried to hook him midbody he jerked and slid off the table and hit the floor with a thud! At least ten business-suited men were suddenly standing at the back of the room! It is now time to come clean about Charlie. He was the subject of some research to find out if the envenomation of a food item is essential to proper digestion in a venomous snake. Consequently, Charlie has had his tubes tied! Wait! The ducts that lead from the venom glands at the base of his jaws to his fangs have been surgically tied. Old Charlie has fangs and venom glands but no ducts.

The well-suited business men slowly returned to their seats. "Hey, I wasn't scared!" Uh huh, right.

Western Massasauga

This dinky denizen lives in a two-hundred-mile band of prairie running from the Gulf Coast to the northeastern Panhandle. There are brown spots along the top and both sides of his body. The belly is mottled with grey-brown. Most adult snakes measure two feet in length. The record is 34.75 inches. They don't like it hot and they will go into a summertime aestivation when it gets above 93 degrees. They are most abundant in late spring, and by July they seem almost nonexistent. They eat lizards, small snakes, frogs, mice, and an occasional shrew.

The young are live-born in July and August. They number from 5 to 15 and are about eight inches long. They are secretive animals and spend most of the daylight hours underground or in a dense clump of prickly pear cactus.

Western Pygmy Rattlesnake

It is the smallest of the Texas rattlesnakes. It is found throughout East Texas from Texarkana through Beaumont. It is not a common snake but seems to be abundant in all the good spots. Its color is grey in the back, spotted with black, with a reddish stripe down the backbone. It has a whitish belly. The rattle, even when he is thoroughly hissed, is no louder than a faint buzzing sound. You should not lean down too close! The adult snake averages no more than 14 to 20 inches, the record being a bit more than 25 inches.

When he sees you, he does all the neat rattlesnake stuff, except for the coiling. He will puff up his body and snap sharply sideways. The strike hardly ever reaches more than a few inches because they do not go into the S-shaped spring-like coil as is characteristic of our other rattlesnakes. It likes to hang around water and enjoys river flood plains, swamps, and wet prairies.

The young are born alive. They are the smallest of the Texas rattlesnake babies measuring only a little over five inches long. Keep in mind that even at that size they will bite. The venom is hemolytic and will affect you accordingly.

Glossary

Aestivation: (1) spending some R and R in Estes Park, Colorado (2) hibernation during the summer

Anaphylaxis: (1) would I use a word like that? Shame on you! (2) An allergic reaction to antivenin

Anterior: (1) the inside of an ant (2) toward the head

Antivenin: (1) people who didn't like this old dude in Russia (2) serum produced from the antibodies of animals injected with snake poison.

Backbone: (1) something snake-haters lose when confronted by a snake (2) snakes have one that numbers as many as 300 bones, you have 33 or 34

Cold-blooded: (1) most traffic cops (2) a body temperature that is regulated by the surrounding air temperature

Constrictor: (1) first date (2) those lovable snakes that hug other animals to death

Ectothermic: see poikilothermic, or cold-blooded

Ecydis: (1) bad spelling of a word that means "everybody leaving at once" (2) all them snakes gotta shed them skins

Fang: (1) something Chinese (2) needle-sharp, hollow teeth found in all poisonous snakes (3) according to most people, they are found in all snakes

Forked-tongue: (1) the white man once used it to speak (2) the condition of the snake tongue allowing it to gather airborne scent particles that, by way of Jacobson's organ in the roof of his mouth, helps him to smell (3) also used by a snake to reach out and touch someone (4) granny says it's a stinger that a snake can use really well

"Forked tongue: (1) the white man once used it to speak."

Huge: any snake

Poison: (1) amber-colored liquid produced from the rear or at either side of the snake's head (2) all snakes

Poikilothermic: (1) Hawaiian high in the heat. I must explain here. You see I like to break up a word and associate its parts thereby making it easy for me to remember. So, poi, a Hawaiian food. Then we have kilo, a drug weight which undoubtedly would get you high (and dead!). Last we see thermic, having to do with temperature. I also have been known to waste a lot of time (2) see ectothermic or cold-blooded

Scales: (1) no other reason for Toledo, Ohio (2) snake covering made of chitin (3) something you don't want to step on in the bathroom

"Scales: (1) no other reason for Toledo, Ohio."

Shed: (1) a good place to find snakes (2) the periodic removal of outer snake skin determined by the animal's age, growth rate, and humidity (3) see ecydis

Slime: (1) most brothers-in-law and some uncles (2) something snakes never had and never will

Snake: (1) long, cylindrical, scale-covered, cold-blooded animals (2) ex-spouses (3) the reason you bought this book

Sneaky: (1) lawyers (2) all snakes (No snake in the world is faster than what it eats. Consequently, it is necessary that it be sneaky!)

Sexual dimorphism: (1) la difference (2) boys are boys and girls are girls and you can tell by looking (3) differences not limited to snakes

Thermoregulation: (1) usually reserved for the head of the household who keeps the key to the thermostat (2) the regulation of body temperature by moving from cool-to-warm-to-cool; snakes do that

Venom: (1) page 73, paragraph 4, line 27 of any divorce decree (2) same as poison but a much worse sounding word

Vent: (1) the name I wanted to give my first child (2) the anus

Scientific Name Index

I learned in seventh grade life science class that every living thing on this earth has seven names. There is a name for each group and the names move from general such as kingdom to very specific such as species. The groups are: Kingdom, Phylum, Class, Order, Family, Genus, and Species. That is hard to memorize so we have this little statement: King Phillip Came Over From Germany Stoned!

Genus Species	*Common Name*	*Page*
Python reticulatus	Reticulated python	93
Regina grahamii	Crayfish snake	13
	Graham's water snake	13
Rhinocheilus lecontei	Longnose snake	36
Salvadora grahamiae	Patchnose snake	41
Sistrurus catenatus	Massasauga rattlesnake	157, 165
Sistrurus malarius	Western pygmy rattlesnake	166
Sonora semiannulata	Ground snake	22
Storeia dekayi	Brown snake	6
	DeKay's snake	6
Tantilla gracilis	Flathead snake	17
Tantilla nigriceps	Blackhead snake	3
Thamnophis marcianus	Garter snake	19
	Grass snake	19
Thamnophis proximus	Western ribbon snake	50
Trimorphodon biscutatus	Texas lyre snake	68
Tropidoclonion lineatum	Lined snake	34
Virginia striatula	Rough earth snake	15
	Ground snake	15

Common Name Index

Common Name	*Genus / Species*	*Page*
Grey-banded king snake	*Lampropeltis alterna*	28
Great Plains rat snake	*Elaphe guttata*	45
Ground snake	*Sonora semiannulata*	22
Highland moccasin	*Agkistrodon contortrix*	71
Hognose snake	*Heterodon platyrhinos*	24
Indigo snake	*Drymarchon corais*	26
Lined snake	*Tropidoclonion lineatum*	34
Longnose snake	*Rhinocheilus lecontei*	36
Massasauga rattlesnake	*Sistrurus catenatus*	158, 165
Mojave rattlesnake	*Crotalus scutulatus*	159
Mottled rock rattlesnake	*Crotalus l. lepidus*	160
Northern cat-eyed snake	*Leptodeira septentrionalis*	67
Patchnose snake	*Salvadora grahamiae*	41
Prairie king snake	*Lampropeltis calligaster*	29
Prairie rattlesnake	*Crotalus veridus*	161
Prairie ringneck snake	*Diadophis punctatus*	52
Prairie runner	*Masticophis flagellum*	10
Reticulated python	*Python reticulatus*	93
Rough earth snake	*Virginia striatula*	15
Rough green tree snake	*Opheodrys aestivus*	54
Slender glass lizard	*Ophisaurus attenuatus*	100
South American boa	*Boa constrictor*	95
Texas coral snake	*Micrurus fulvius*	74
Texas lyre snake	*Trimorphodon biscutatus*	68

Bibliography

Conant, R. *A Field Guide to the Reptiles and Amphibians of Eastern and Central North America*. 2d Ed. Boston: Houghton Mifflin Co., 1974.

Klauber, L.M. *Rattlesnakes, their Habits, Life Histories and Influence on Mankind*. 2d Ed. 2 vols. Berkeley: University of California Press, 1972.

Mehrtens, John M. *Living Snakes of the World*. Dorset, England: Sterling Publishing Co., Inc., 1987.

Tennant, Alan. *A Field Guide to Texas Snakes*. Austin: Texas Monthly Press, 1985.

Werler, John E. *Poisonous Snakes of Texas*. Bulletin No. 31, Austin: Texas Parks and Wildlife, 1978.

Wright, Albert Hazen and Wright, Anna Allen. *Handbook of Snakes of the United States and Canada*. Ithaca, New York: Comstock Publishing Associates, Cornell University Press, 1957.

The End